Sunset
Children's Furniture

By the Editors of Sunset Books and Sunset Magazine

Lane Publishing Co. • Menlo Park, California

Book Editors
Scott Fitzgerrell
Don Vandervort

Developmental Editor
Fran Feldman

Contributing Editor
Scott Atkinson

Coordinating Editor
Michael Green

Design
Roger Flanagan

Illustrations
Bill Oetinger

Photography
Stephen Marley

Photo Stylist
JoAnn Masaoka

Just for kids...

All children love a place that's theirs alone—a special realm where everything is child-size, where dreams, imagination, and whimsy hold sway. The best furnishings and playthings for children reflect the spirit, as well as the scale, of that magical world.

If you've always wanted to create something special for a child—a piece of furniture or a plaything that combines charm and fancy with practicality and good craftsmanship—this is the book for you. Here, we present a delightful array of one-of-a-kind woodworking designs just right for a child-size world.

Whether you're an experienced woodworker or an enthusiastic beginner, there's a project here for you. From the simple and lovable rocking lion to the stylish teen bed-desk-wardrobe combination, you're sure to find a design among the more than 30 on these pages that's both tailored to your skills and a perfect fit for the special child you have in mind.

There's plenty here to inspire you, but we don't leave you up in the clouds—we offer down-to-earth, practical information, too. A complete materials list accompanies each project, and detailed instructions and drawings guide you each step of the way, from cutting out the pieces to painting on the last curlicue. In addition, special features scattered throughout the book tell you all about the tools, materials, and techniques you'll need to complete the projects.

We hope you'll derive many hours of pleasure from building these projects, and that you'll think of our book as your partner in creating something truly special. We supply the plans; you supply what money can't buy—the time,

the talent, and most importantly, the loving touch.

We gratefully acknowledge the many woodworkers who helped us test projects and prepare them for the camera—especially John Jones of J & W Wood Products, David Pederson, Phil Puccinelli, Peter Santulli, Paul Staley of Modern Cabinet Systems, and Jim Thomson. For their generosity in sharing props for use in our photographs, we thank Bear Comforts, Cotton Works, The Dollhouse Factory, The Hammock Way, Palo Alto Sport Shop & Toy World, Strouds Linen Warehouse, Toyhouse Schoolhouse, Velveteen Rabbit, and Wherehouse for Bedspreads. We also extend special thanks to copy editor Scott Lowe and photographic assistant Greg Anderson.

Cover: Pulled up front-and-center is our snappy Race Car Bed (page 82); beyond, the elegant Heirloom Rocking Horse (page 8) stands saddled and ready to ride. The Modular Wall System (page 39) provides a place for everything and keeps everything in its place. Photograph by Stephen Marley. Cover design by JoAnn Masaoka.

Editor, Sunset Books: David E. Clark

First printing May 1985

CONTENTS

Delight a young artist with this
easy-to-build Folding Easel (page 15).

Special features

Childscale

Few pleasures compare with that of making something special for a child you love. If you're a woodworker—or would like to be—you're in an enviable position: the satisfaction you derive from your hobby can go hand in hand with the pleasure you'll get from delighting that child.

Children live in a world of adult-scale furnishings, furnishings that don't fit them either physically or psychologically. Even very young children need—and appreciate—furnishings scaled to their growing bodies and minds.

This book can help. It's a collection of child-scale projects—both furniture and playthings—designed to meet the needs of children. But we haven't thought only of pleasing them: everything in the book has been selected to appeal to the woodworker as well as the child. After all, homemade projects should be fun for the builder, too.

Most of the projects were created especially for this book, and we applied a test to each one before including it: either it had to save money over its commercial counterpart or it had to be unavailable commercially.

In addition, we felt that the projects should address a broad range of woodworking abilities, though none should demand professional expertise. For this reason, you'll find a considerable range in the amount of time, talent, and financial resources required to complete the projects.

A brief overview of all the projects in the book, as well as the special features, follows. Also, be sure to note the hints we give on the facing page about how to use the book.

About the projects

 Tailoring furniture to a child's physical needs is a bit like trying to hit a moving target, since children are constantly changing. You can build items that fit a certain range of ages, you can make more specialized things that can be set aside or passed on when outgrown, or you can build furniture and toys that are adjustable and grow with the child. You'll find examples of all three approaches among the projects in this book.

Tailoring to a child's marvelous sense of magic and wonder deserves equal attention. In selecting and designing projects for this book, we made sure to stock it well with imagination and magic.

The book begins with a selection of playthings and room accessories—projects that are part furniture, part toy. The rocking lion and horse (pages 6–9) exemplify the book's range within a single subject: the lion is quick and easy to build, the horse takes longer and requires more skill.

You'll find a customized van toybox and a finely crafted wooden wagon paired up on pages 22–25. The former is easy to build; the latter is more involved, but like the horse, it's an heirloom that's well worth the time and effort it requires.

The animal-shaped chairs on pages 34–35 are pure whimsy—an easily built set of simple chairs made from a single sheet of plywood and some pieces of solid lumber. Less fanciful, but no less practical, are the fold-down stepstool

and the versatile multiposition chair on pages 30–33.

The easel (pages 14–15) and the workbench (pages 26–27) are quick, inexpensive projects designed to give years of service. The play kitchen and doll house cabinets (pages 18–21) work as hard as they play, and each can be used for storage after it's outgrown.

The sports rack, mirrored organizer, and clothes rack on pages 10–13 are all business (but not at the expense of attractive design), and each is easy to build.

The modular wall and closet systems (pages 38–41) offer plenty of organization at minimal expense. Their elegant, uncluttered designs will complement any child's room.

Two sharply contrasting playsets come next. The hardwood table and stools (pages 42–43) are simple, clean, and contemporary; the charming country styling of the painted table, bench, and chairs on pages 46–49 recalls an earlier day. Both projects are easy to build.

Two folk-art cradles follow on pages 50–53. These designs embody the timeless traditions of Scandinavian and Shaker craftsmanship. Each requires a modest store of tools and experience. In contrast, the all-in-one sleep and play structure on pages 54–57 is an easy project designed to be a complete "environment" for a young child.

On pages 58–61 you'll find a pair of contemporary bunk beds. The first unstacks into individual twin beds; the second features an adjustable desk within its L-shaped configuration. Both projects fall into the easy-to-moderate

Building furniture & playthings for children

skill range and both are less expensive than equivalent commercially produced furniture.

If your child sleeps in a metal-framed twin bed, try dressing it up with a little headboard magic—or enhance its usefulness with underbed drawers; the projects on pages 62–65 show you how. If you'd rather start from scratch, consider the chest bed on pages 66–69; within its twin-size frame you can store the contents of a large dresser.

Canopy beds are perennial favorites, and the one on pages 70–71 is no exception. It's also an exceptional value—easy to build and quite inexpensive.

Three fantasy beds are next. On pages 74–77, budding astronauts will find a craft suitable for night flights into dreamland—a space shuttle built from plywood and plastic planters. The tent-topped wagon bed on pages 78–81 evokes everything from a campground to a circus wagon. For the speed demon in your midst, there's the race car bed on pages 82–85. Its startlingly authentic lines will make it look like it's setting lap records right in the middle of your child's room.

An easy-to-build loft bed with desk and wardrobe follows this trio (pages 86–89). Especially effective for a small room, it combines sleep, study, and storage functions in a sleek, stylish package that takes up very little floor space.

The book concludes with three adjustable projects that combine to make a "room that grows up" (pages 90–95). There's a table that can be positioned at three different heights, a convertible crib-to-youth bed with dresser, and a two-position desk. All three share a clean, contemporary look and require moderate woodworking skill; all will save you money over equivalent commercial designs.

About the special features

 Throughout the book you'll find a series of special features beginning with the selection and purchase of materials and ending with finishing. Though it's beyond the scope of this book to offer a complete course in basic woodworking, these features will orient you if you're a beginner and jog your memory if you're an expert. Each one is tailored to the projects in the book.

In "Basic materials" (pages 16–17), we discuss the materials recommended for the projects and guide you in their purchase. "Tools of the trade" (pages 28–29) helps you through the numerous choices you'll need to make when acquiring and using tools. In "Marking, cutting & drilling" (pages 36–37) you'll find many useful tips that will aid you in building your project.

"Joinery" (pages 44–45) is an outline account of a craft within a craft: the creation and assembly of wood joints, connections that are crucial to the structural integrity of the project.

Since some wood joints can be very difficult to make, we've restricted the types of joints used in our projects to the simpler ones. These are all accounted for here.

The final feature, "Finishing your project" (pages 72–73), is a guide to the finishes we used on the projects, as shown in the photographs. These finishes are both easy to apply and extremely durable.

In this feature we explain the techniques you'll need to know, including how to prepare the wood, how to apply each of the various finishes, and how to cut and attach plastic laminate.

Using this book

 After you've decided on a project, read all the instructions and study the illustrations and materials list before starting to build. We've designed these elements to streamline your work: you can shop directly from the list, and the alphabetical labels on the pieces will help you move back and forth between the instructions, the drawings, and the list without any confusion.

Look up any unfamiliar operations in the special features. If you don't have all the tools you need, borrow or rent what you lack. Or consider buying new tools that you can use again and again. Enrolling in an adult education program in woodworking, if it's available in your community, offers an excellent solution to the problem of an inadequate workshop or tool kit.

Once you've marshalled your resources and you understand the procedures, you're ready to begin. Turn the page—and have fun!

These two spirited mounts are off and running. The rocking lion is so quick and easy to build that even young lion tamers can help with construction. The rocking horse is a solid hardwood heirloom that requires more time and effort. Each is a sturdy design and will carry its rider many miles.

Rocking lion

Much like its jungle counterpart, this time-tested rocking lion rarely fails to capture the imaginations of young and old alike. This project can be turned out in a few hours—and a child can help, too.

1. Cut all pieces to size. (Note: The lengths given for neck pieces **D** and **E**, which are cut at a 45° angle at one end, are for the longest sides.) Cut the tops of ends **A** to a 4⅝-inch radius and cut the arches between the legs as shown. Cut twenty-eight 2-inch and twelve 3-inch lengths of dowel. Mark and drill ⅜-inch holes in body pieces **B** as shown.

2. Starting at the top of ends **A**, attach pieces **B** with 2-inch dowels and glue. Use the holes in **B** as guides for drilling corresponding holes in **A**, keeping ends **A** parallel to each other and perpendicular to pieces **B**.

3. Rip the rounded edges from head pieces **C**, then join them by gluing and clamping. Cut the profiles in the head. Glue and nail pieces **D** and **E** to **C**.

4. Drill ⅜-inch head mounting holes in front end **A**. Hold the head in position and drill corresponding holes in **D** and **E**. Attach the head with glue and 3-inch dowels.

5. Cut rockers **F** as shown in the detail drawing; drill the top front mounting hole in each. Mark and drill a corresponding hole in each leg of front end **A** and temporarily assemble with dowels. Clamp the rear legs to the rockers and adjust the body until level. Drill the remaining mounting holes and fasten rockers **F** to legs **A** with glue and dowels.

6. Trim the dowels, round over all edges, and sand. Attach the pulls with glue and dowels. Finish, coloring the nose and eyes with a pen. Nail on the mane and attach the tail (pass it through a 1-inch hole drilled in back end **A**).

Design: Rick Morrall.

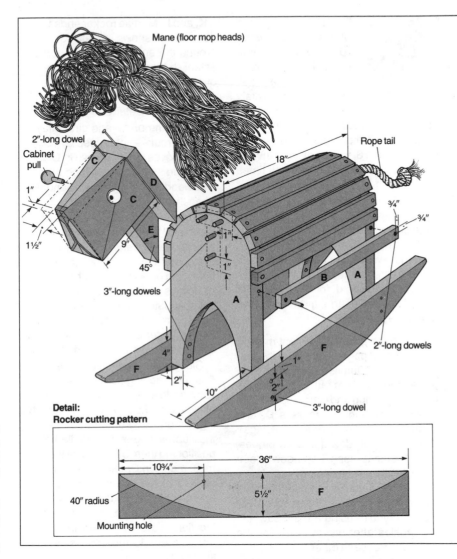

Detail:
Rocker cutting pattern

BUY		TO MAKE		
Clear fir				
1	3-foot 2 by 10	2	Ends **A**:	1½″ by 9¼″ by 16″
1	16-foot 1 by 2	10	Body pieces **B**:	¾″ by 1½″ by 18″
1	6-foot 1 by 2	3	Body pieces **B**:	¾″ by 1½″ by 18″
1	8-foot 2 by 6	2	Head pieces **C**:	1½″ by 5½″ by 9″
		2	Rockers **F**:	1½″ by 5½″ by 36″
1	2-foot 2 by 4	1	Neck piece **D**:	1½″ by 3½″ by 9½″
		1	Neck piece **E**:	1½″ by 3½″ by 7½″

MISCELLANEOUS

8′ of ⅜″ hardwood dowel • 2′ of 1″ braided rope • 2 floor mop heads
10d nails • 2 wood cabinet pulls • Wood glue • Clear nontoxic finish • Black felt-tip pen

Heirloom rocking horse

The simple elegance of this fine hardwood rocking horse will make it a source of delight for all ages. If you're a moderately experienced woodworker, you won't find the project difficult. The beauty and durability of the completed horse, pictured on page 6, will repay your investment in time and materials many times over.

In addition to basic tools, you'll need a saber saw, router, and a radial-arm or table saw to build the horse as shown; a band saw and belt sander are helpful. Both the level of difficulty and the tools needed are somewhat "adjustable," however; you could, for example, omit the inlaid bridle and girth—and the router they require.

1. Using the grid-enlargement method described on page 36, transfer the cutting patterns (Details 1 and 3) to heavy paper and cut them out. Edge-join the boards by gluing and clamping to make "blanks" for body **A**, rockers **D**, and saddle halves **J** (see detail drawings). Cut the ⅜-inch dowel into 40 pieces, each 1½ inches long. Blind dowel (see page 45) the body blank where shown in Detail 3. If you're not using a band saw, cut the saddle-half profiles before gluing; if you're using a band saw, cut the profiles after gluing. (Be sure the halves mirror each other.)

Pieces **K** and **L** and the optional bridle and girth inlays are ¼ inch thick. Rip these pieces from a dark hardwood (ours are walnut), or use ash or oak and stain it darker.

Trace the patterns for body **A**, legs **B** and **C** (made from single boards), and saddle halves **J**, then cut all pieces. Use a beam compass or, preferably, the saber-saw jig shown on page 36 to cut the rocker blank as shown in Detail 2; move the pivot point up 3¼ inches for each cut. Add reinforcing dowels to the feet and rockers where shown and shape the rocker ends. Cut pieces **E**–

I, **K**, and **L**. Mortise rocker ends ¼ inch deep where shown in Detail 3, tracing around the end of a foot support **E** to establish the size; be sure the centers of the mortises are 32 inches apart. Cut the four leg wedges from the 1 by 6 as shown in Detail 3.

To add the bridle and girth inlays, if desired, rout ³⁄₁₆-inch-deep by ¾-inch-wide grooves where shown in Detail 3; then glue ¼-inch by ¾-inch strips of hardwood in each groove. Sand flush when the glue has cured.

2. Unless otherwise indicated, assemble all the pieces with glue and the appropriate screws as shown in the exploded drawing. Drill counterbore holes and plug with screw hole buttons or dowels as indicated. Be careful to drill adequate shank-clearance and pilot holes to avoid splitting the hardwood. Before assembling the horse, round over all exposed edges and sand.

Glue the leg wedges in place on legs **B** and **C**, aligning as shown in Detail 3. (Be sure to keep the left and right pairs of legs sorted as you work.) Place two legs on one side of the body, sanding their upper edges so they lie flat and positioning them by means of the alignment marks in Detail 3. Check that the centers of the hooves are 32 inches apart; then fasten the legs in place, observing the right or left-side screw locations as shown. Add the two remaining legs to the other side in the same way.

3. Assemble rockers **D** and foot supports **E**. Add footrests **F**, gluing and doweling them in place as shown in Detail 3 and the exploded drawing. If your buckaroo needs a booster step, build it by gluing and doweling step **G** to supports **H**; use screws and two pieces **I** to lock the step assembly in place. Center the horse on the supports and screw the feet to the foot supports as shown.

4. Fasten one saddle half **J** to the body with 1½-inch screws, then add its mate, using 2½ and 3-inch screws (see exploded drawing and Detail 1). Glue and clamp the two remaining pieces **I** to the horse's head to act as mounts for the leather ears. Drill holes in mounts **I** where shown. Glue and clamp trim pieces **K** and **L** in position. Add ½-inch screw hole buttons for eyes. Round one end of each of the 1-inch dowel handles and drill the other end as shown. Drill holes in **A** and **K** (see Detail 3). Use the threaded rod to connect the handles and body.

5. Shape and sand the saddle, using the photo as a guide. Do any final shaping, rounding, and finish sanding, then apply two or three coats of varnish or penetrating oil finish. Cut and roll the leather ears, insert them in ear mounts **I**, and secure them with toothpicks glued in ¹⁄₁₆-inch holes drilled through the mounts and ears.

Design: Louis Jewell.

BUY		TO MAKE	
Ash, oak, or walnut			
18	board feet of ¾-inch stock	Pieces **A–D**, **H**, and **J–L** (see text and drawings for sizes)	
		2 Foot supports **E**: ¾″ by 2″ by 14½″	
		3 Footrests **F**: ¾″ by 2″ by 15½″	
		1 Step **G**: ¾″ by 2″ by 14″	
		4 Pieces **I**: ¾″ by ¾″ by 2½″	

MISCELLANEOUS

6′ of ⅜″ hardwood dowel • 2 pieces of 1″ hardwood dowel, each 3″ long
24 sq. inches of leather • Screw hole buttons: 20 at ⅜″, 2 at ½″
4′ of 1 by 6 pine or fir • 2 round toothpicks • 4½″ of ¼″ threaded rod • Wood glue
#12 flathead woodscrews: 24 at 1½″, 4 at 1¾″, 1 at 2½″, 3 at 3″ • Finish

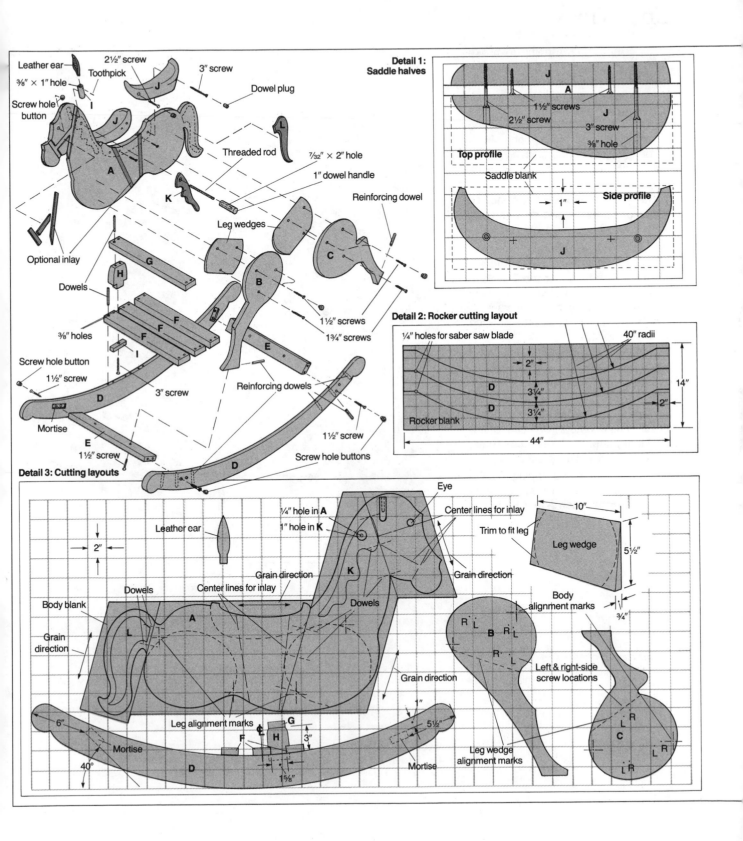

Leather ear
⅜" × 1" hole
Screw hole button

2½" screw
Toothpick
I
J

3" screw
Dowel plug

J

J

A

Dowel plug
L

Threaded rod
⁷⁄₃₂" × 2" hole
1" dowel handle

K

Leg wedges

Reinforcing dowel

C

Optional inlay

G

Dowels

H

B

⅜" holes

F
F
F
F

I

E

1½" screws
1¾" screws

Screw hole button
1½" screw

3" screw

D

Reinforcing dowels

Mortise

E
1½" screw

D

1½" screw

Screw hole buttons

Detail 1:
Saddle halves

J

A

J

1½" screws
2½" screw
3" screw
⅜" hole

Top profile
Saddle blank

1"

Side profile

J

Detail 2: Rocker cutting layout

¼" holes for saber saw blade
40" radii

2"

D
3¼"
D
3¼"

Rocker blank

14"

2"

44"

Detail 3: Cutting layouts

Eye
¼" hole in **A**
1" hole in **K**

Center lines for inlay

Leather ear

2"

Grain direction
Dowels
Center lines for inlay

Body blank

Grain direction

K

A

L

Dowels

Grain direction

Trim to fit leg

10"

Leg wedge

5½"

Body alignment marks

¾"

R L
B R L

R L

Left & right-side screw locations

6"

Mortise

40°

F

H
G

D

3"

1⅝"

5½"

1"

Mortise

Leg wedge alignment marks

Leg alignment marks

R
L

C

L R

L R

FORM & FUNCTION

Sports rack (below)
Mirrored organizer (page 12)
Freestanding clothes rack (page 13)

Sports rack

This easy-to-make rack keeps the clutter of sports equipment out of closet corners. Baseball bats dangle from pegs, skis and other long items stand upright, shoes go on shelves, sports clothing hangs from pegs, and balls are stored in the base.

The perfect project for a novice woodworker, this sports rack requires only basic tools and skills for its construction.

1. Cut all pieces to size. Mark and drill 1½-inch-deep holes for the dowels in top **C** where shown. Cut the angle along sides **A** as shown in the detail drawing. Cut the dowel into eight pieces, each 5½ inches long.

2. Glue and nail sides **A** to base **B** and top **C**. Add shelves **D** and front **E**. Glue one end of each dowel and tap them into the holes in **C**.

3. Set the nails and fill the holes. Sand all surfaces and apply one coat of finish. Lightly sand the inner face of back **F** and recoat it. Let the pieces dry.

4. Nail on the back, dropping it down ¾ inch from the upper edge of top **C** and overlapping each side **A** ⅜ inch.

Design: Don Vandervort.

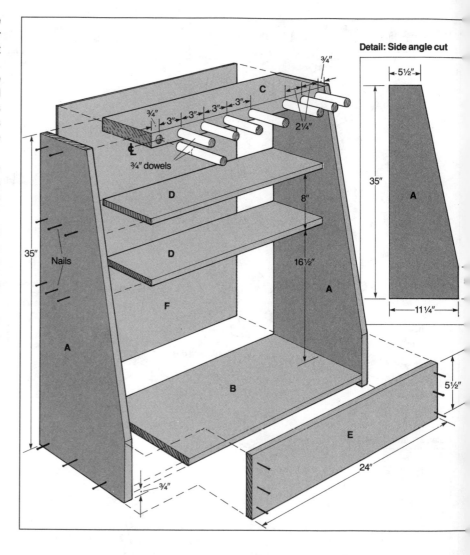

Detail: Side angle cut

BUY		TO MAKE		
Knotty (#3) pine				
1	8-foot 1 by 12	2	Sides **A**:	¾" by 11¼" by 35"
		1	Base **B**:	¾" by 11¼" by 22½"
1	6-foot 1 by 6	2	Shelves **D**:	¾" by 5½" by 22½"
		1	Front **E**:	¾" by 5½" by 24"
1	2-foot 2 by 6	1	Top **C**:	1½" by 5½" by 22½"
Hardboard				
1	¼-inch 2 by 4-foot piece	1	Back **F**:	¼" by 23¼" by 33⅛"

MISCELLANEOUS

4' of ¾" hardwood dowel • 5d finishing nails • Wood glue • Wood putty
Clear satin polyurethane finish

Practical, good-looking, and easily built accessories include (from left to right) a sports rack, a mirrored organizer, and a clothes rack. Each is made from standard-dimension pine and requires little more than basic tools.

11

Mirrored organizer

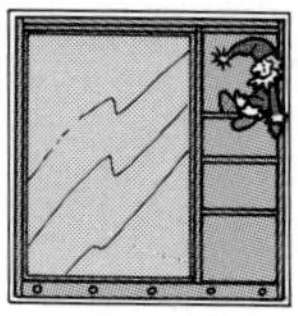

This simple, wall-mounted unit (see photo on page 11) offers a mirror, shelves for display or organization, and pegs for backpacks, jackets, and the like. The case, made from standard-dimension lumber, is glued and screwed together. Order the mirror from a glass dealer before you begin the case.

Cut the plugs for the screw holes from scrap lumber, using a plug cutter.

1. Cut all pieces to size. Cut the dowel into five pieces, each 3½ inches long. Mark and drill 1-inch-deep holes for the dowels in base **B** where shown.

2. Drill counterbore and pilot holes for screws. Glue all joints. Using 1¼-inch screws, join sides **A** to base **B** and top **C**. Screw divider **D** in place, spacing it from the right side with shelves **E** (use two 2½-inch screws to attach **D** to base **B**). Attach the shelves, screwing through **A** and **D** as shown.

3. Using glue and brads, attach back **F**, leaving a ¼-inch border all around. Glue one end of each dowel and tap the dowels into the holes in base **B**.

4. Glue and screw mounting strips **G** and **H** against the back, screwing down through top **C** with 1¼-inch screws.

5. Plug the screw holes. Sand and finish all the wood, including the quarter-round molding.

6. With the unit on its back, set the mirror in place. Cut the quarter-round to fit around the mirror, mitering the ends. Carefully toenail the pieces with brads. Set the heads and fill the holes.

7. Drill countersink and pilot holes through mounting strips **G** and **H** and screw the unit to wall studs, using two 2½-inch screws.

Design: Don Vandervort.

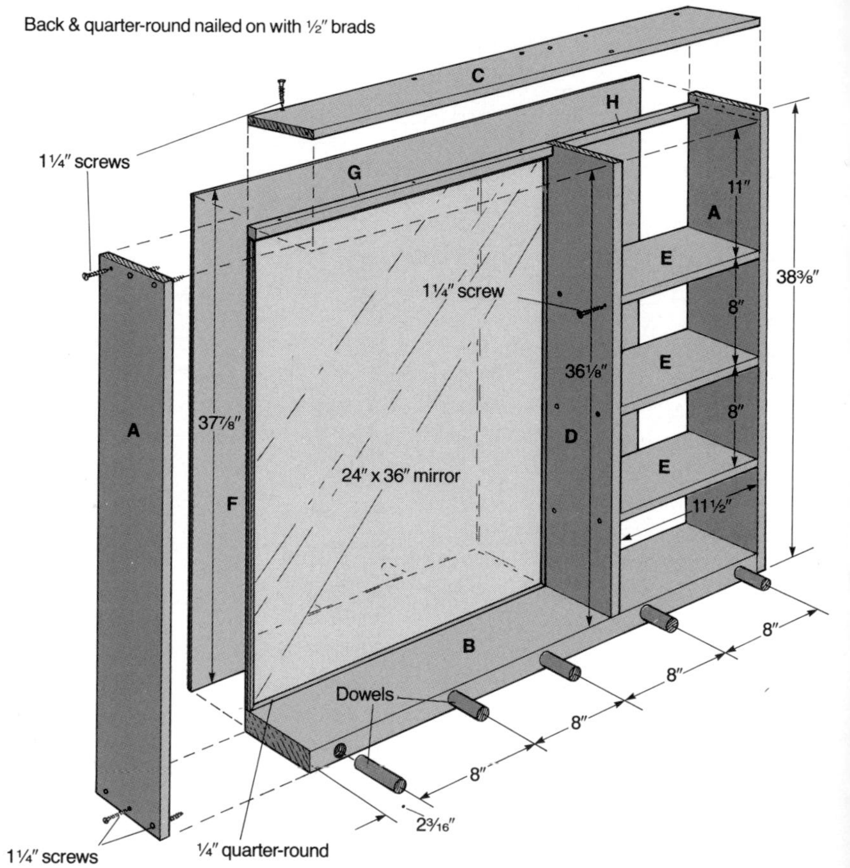
Back & quarter-round nailed on with ½″ brads
C
H
G
1¼″ screws
A
11″
38⅜″
E
1¼″ screw
8″
E
36⅛″
8″
37⅞″
A
D
E
24″ x 36″ mirror
F
11½″
B
8″
8″
Dowels
8″
8″
2³⁄₁₆″
1¼″ screws
¼″ quarter-round

BUY		TO MAKE
Clear pine		
1	10-foot 1 by 6	2 Sides **A**: ¾″ by 5½″ by 38⅜″ 1 Top **C**: ¾″ by 5½″ by 36⅜″
1	8-foot 1 by 6	1 Divider **D**: ¾″ by 5½″ by 36⅛″ 3 Shelves **E**: ¾″ by 5½″ by 11½″
1	4-foot 2 by 6	1 Base **B**: 1½″ by 5½″ by 36⅜″
1	3-foot 1 by 1	1 Mounting strip **G**: ½″ by ¾″ by 24⅛″ 1 Mounting strip **H**: ½″ by ¾″ by 11½″
Birch plywood (shop grade)		
1	¼-inch 4 by 4-foot sheet	1 Back **F**: ¼″ by 37⅜″ by 37⅞″

MISCELLANEOUS

¼″ by 24″ by 36″ mirror • 12′ of ¼″ quarter-round clear pine molding
31 1¼″ by #6 drywall screws • 4 2½″ by #6 drywall screws • ½″ brads • Wood glue
Wood putty • Clear satin polyurethane finish • 2′ of ¾″ hardwood dowel

Freestanding clothes rack

Add a decorative element and plenty of additional storage to a child's room with this freestanding clothes rack, pictured on page 11. It offers a 3½-foot closet pole and two shelves—one below for shoes and skates, and one above for books, toys, and other treasures.

Because construction is so simple, a child can help you build the rack. In addition to basic tools, you'll need a saber saw or band saw for making the curved cuts. A router is helpful for rounding over edges.

1. Cut the pieces to size. Using the grid-enlargement method described on page 36, cut out feet **E** and hearts **F** (see detail drawing) and round over their edges. Sand the curves smooth. If you wish to finish the feet and hearts to contrast with the frame, as shown in the photo, stain them now.

2. Glue and screw all joints; countersink the screws. Attach top **B** to sides **A**, then attach sides **A** to base **C** and shelf **D**. Fasten shelf **D** to base **C**. Mount the closet pole brackets where shown. Cut the fir round to fit between the closet pole brackets and install it.

3. Fill all holes and sand the unfinished pieces. Finish all pieces, including the feet and hearts, with the clear finish of your choice.

4. Using three screws for each foot, glue and screw on the feet, starting the screws from the inside of sides **A**; be careful not to countersink the screws too deeply. Attach the hearts in the same manner.

Design: Heidi Merry.

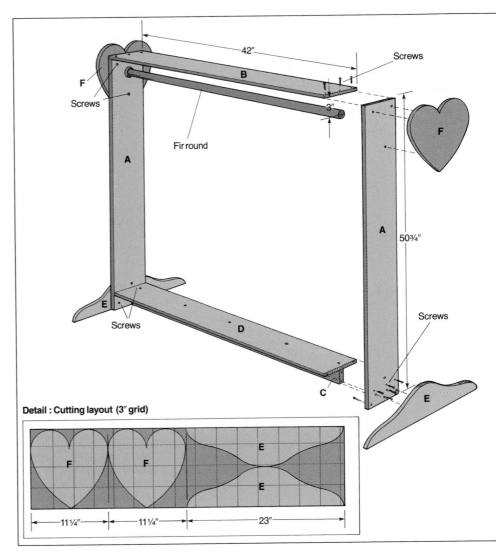

Detail : Cutting layout (3″ grid)

BUY		TO MAKE		
Knotty (#3) pine				
2	6-foot 1 by 8s	2	Sides **A**:	¾″ by 7¼″ by 50″
		1	Top **B**:	¾″ by 7¼″ by 42″
1	4-foot 1 by 8	1	Shelf **D**:	¾″ by 7¼″ by 40½″
1	4-foot 1 by 4	1	Base **C**:	¾″ by 3½″ by 40½″
1	4-foot 1 by 12	2	Feet **E**	(see detail drawing)
		2	Hearts **F**	(see detail drawing)

MISCELLANEOUS
33 drywall screws, 1¼″ by #6 • 4′ of 1⅜″ fir round • 1 pair closet pole brackets with screws
Wood glue • Wood putty • Maple stain • Clear finish

To paint a masterpiece, every artist needs the right equipment. This sturdy, versatile easel fills the bill—and it's equally well adapted to chalk and marker work. As the inset photos show, the easel folds up compactly once the masterpiece is finished.

Folding easel

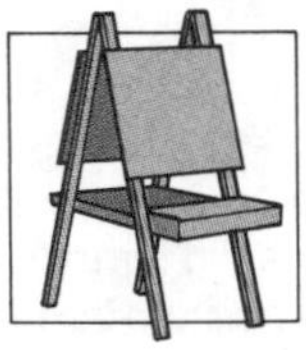

Young artists will like this versatile easel: its adjustable art boards provide generous space for creativity, and its large tray holds plenty of chalk, paint, and markers. Parents will appreciate its easy-to-build folding design: the easel is compact when folded and rigid when set up.

1. Cut all pieces to size. Mark and drill holes for pivot screws in tray sides **A** and two legs **E**; mark and drill holes for locking dowels in remaining legs **E** (see Details 1 and 2). Drill holes in one crosspiece **C** as shown. Cut the dowel in half.

2. Join tray sides **A** and **B** with glue and 6d nails spaced 3 inches apart. Add crosspieces **C**, using glue and 4d nails. Set the nails and fill the holes. Cut the molding in half and glue in place where shown. Attach tray bottom **D** with glue and 2d nails, leaving a ¼-inch border all around.

3. Join legs **E** in pairs with hinges. Round over all wood edges, sand, and apply two coats of gloss polyurethane to all wood pieces, tray bottom, and one art board **F**. Paint the other board with chalkboard paint.

4. Attach the legs to tray sides **A** with 1½-inch screws and finish washers, leaving the screws just loose enough to permit easy movement. Glue the dowels in opposite legs (see Detail 1).

5. Stand the easel up and open the legs, resting the tray on the dowels. When the tray is level, mark the outline of each dowel on the tray underside. Cut away the tray within the outlines with a craft knife or chisel. Install the mending plates as shown in Detail 1 (they should pivot to lock and unlock the dowels in their notches). Using ¾-inch screws, attach art boards **F** and chalkboard spacers **G** to the legs as shown, setting their height as desired.

Design: Scott Fitzgerrell.

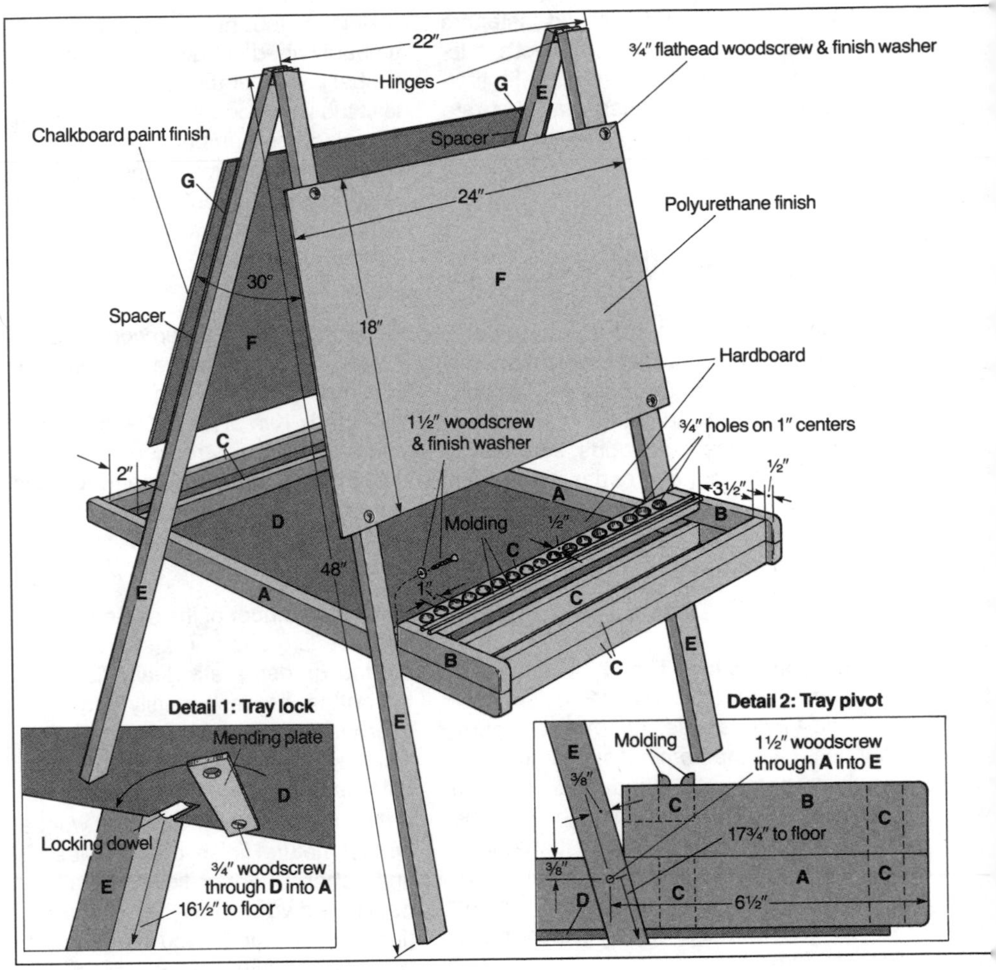
22"
Hinges
G
E
¾" flathead woodscrew & finish washer
Chalkboard paint finish
Spacer
G
24"
Polyurethane finish
30°
F
Spacer
F
18"
Hardboard
1½" woodscrew & finish washer
¾" holes on 1" centers
C
½"
2"
3½"
A
B
D
Molding
½"
C
48"
1"
E
A
C
E
B
C
Detail 1: Tray lock
Mending plate
D
Locking dowel
E
¾" woodscrew through D into A
16½" to floor
E
Detail 2: Tray pivot
Molding
1½" woodscrew through A into E
E
⅜"
C
B
C
17¾" to floor
⅜"
C
A
C
D
6½"

BUY		TO MAKE
Clear fir or pine		
4	8-foot 1 by 2s	2 Tray sides **A**: ¾" by 1½" by 28"
		2 Tray sides **B**: ¾" by 1½" by 6¼"
		6 Tray crosspieces **C**: ¾" by 1½" by 17½"
		4 Legs **E**: ¾" by 1½" by 48"
Tempered hardboard		
1	¼-inch 4 by 4-foot sheet	1 Tray bottom **D**: ¼" by 18½" by 26½"
		2 Art boards **F**: ¼" by 18" by 24"
		2 Chalkboard spacers **G**: ¼" by 1½" by 18"

MISCELLANEOUS

3' of ¼" quarter-round molding • 3" of ¼" hardwood dowel
10 brass flathead woodscrews, ¾" by #8, with finish washers
2 1½" butt hinges with screws • 2 brass flathead woodscrews, 1½" by #8, with finish washers
2d, 4d, and 6d finishing nails • 2 mending plates, ¾" by 1½"
Wood glue • Wood putty • Chalkboard paint • Gloss polyurethane finish

BASIC MATERIALS

Though quality lumber and fasteners alone won't ensure a project's success, it's difficult to come up with first-rate results using less than first-rate materials. Here's a guide to choosing the best.

Shopping for lumber

Lumber is divided into softwoods and hardwoods, terms that refer to the origin of the wood. Hardwoods, such as ash, birch, maple, and oak, come from deciduous trees; softwoods, such as fir, pine, redwood, and cedar, come from conifers. As a rule, softwoods are less expensive and more readily available. (To find hardwoods, look in the Yellow Pages under "Hardwoods.")

Lumber sizing. Though it's often assumed that a 2 by 4 is 2 inches thick and 4 inches wide, it's not. These numbers give the *nominal* size of the lumber—before it's dried and surfaced (planed). The chart at right lists the nominal sizes of softwood lumber and the standard surfaced dimensions for each. The lumber is sold in lengths ranging from 6 to 20 feet in increments of 2 feet.

Buying hardwoods can be tricky; they usually come in random widths and lengths, in odd thicknesses, and often with rough edges. You may see the designations S1S, S2S, S3S, and S4S, which mean "surfaced one side," "surfaced two sides," and so on. The term "four-quarter," or 4/4, represents the nominal thickness of a board. An unsurfaced 4/4 board is between 1 and 1¼ inches thick, an 8/4 board around 2 inches thick, and so on. The surfaced size will be somewhat less.

Unless you have a planer, you'll probably need to have your hardwood lumber milled at the lumberyard. And to fit the wood on hand, you may need to resize your lumber slightly or fine-tune the project dimensions. For minor resizing jobs, a table saw equipped with a carbide-tipped blade is usually sufficient.

Moisture content. When wood is sawn, it's still "green." Before it's ready to use, most lumber is either air-dried or kiln-dried. Kiln-drying, the more expensive process, reduces moisture content to less than 8 percent. To avoid warping or shrinking, use kiln-dried lumber whenever possible.

Grading. Lumber of the same species and size is graded on a sliding scale: the top grades are virtually flawless, the bottom grades virtually unusable. Even within the same grade, you'll often find striking differences between pieces. Let your eye be the final judge.

If you're using softwood and want a perfect, natural finish, choose Clear, B and better, Superior finish, Clear all-heart (redwood only), or Supreme (Idaho white pine). If you plan to paint, you can substitute a less expensive wood, since paint hides many defects. Number 2 and 3 pines are often chosen specifically for their tight knot patterns.

Top hardwood grades include Firsts, Seconds, and a mix of the two called FAS. Next comes Select. Between FAS and Select are two subgrades: FAS 1 face and Select and better. The former, graded FAS on one face but No. 1 Common (the next lower grade) on the other, may be an economical choice if only one side will show.

Choosing plywood

Plywood, a man-made product, offers several advantages over solid lumber: exceptional strength, availability in large sheets, and, in most cases, lower cost.

Softwood plywood. Though softwood plywood may be manufactured from up to 70 species, Douglas fir and Southern pine are the most common. The standard sheet size is 4 by 8 feet, but many lumberyards sell half sheets.

Both the face and the back of a plywood panel are graded by appearance (letters A through D designate the standard grades). Generally, an A face is suitable for a natural finish, a B face for stain, and a repaired C face (called "C-plugged") for paint. If both sides of a panel will be exposed, use AB plywood. An AD panel is an economical choice where only one side will show.

Standard dimensions of surfaced lumber

NOMINAL SIZE	SURFACED (Actual Size)
1 by 2	¾" by 1½"
1 by 3	¾" by 2½"
1 by 4	¾" by 3½"
1 by 6	¾" by 5½"
1 by 8	¾" by 7¼"
1 by 10	¾" by 9¼"
1 by 12	¾" by 11¼"
2 by 3	1½" by 2½"
2 by 4	1½" by 3½"
2 by 6	1½" by 5½"
2 by 8	1½" by 7¼"
2 by 10	1½" by 9¼"
2 by 12	1½" by 11¼"
4 by 4	3½" by 3½"

Hardwood plywood. Popular domestic hardwood plywoods include ash, birch, black walnut, cherry, maple, and oak. A number of imported woods are also available. We've selected birch for many of the projects; it's durable and attractive, tools cleanly, and is one of the lowest-priced hardwood plywoods. You can increase your savings by using "shop grade" birch plywood—panels with very slight defects that won't meet grading standards. Standard panel size is 4 by 8 feet.

If you're planning to clear-finish plywood edges or simply looking for extra strength in thin sheets, opt for Baltic or Finnish plywood, birch panels made up of many very thin, solid veneers. They're available in 5 by 5 or 8 by 4-foot sheets (the grain runs across the width).

Hardwood plywoods have their own grades: Premium, the top of the line, is the best choice for a natural finish. Good grade (sometimes designated "Number 1") normally looks best when stained. Sound grade (Number 2) is best when painted. Grades lower than Sound are generally not worth using.

Fasteners

Nails, screws, bolts, and adhesives —these fasteners hold together all the other materials featured in the projects. Here's a closer look at each.

Nails. *Box* nails have wide, flat heads to spread the load and resist pull-through. When you don't want the nail's head to show, use a *finishing* nail and sink the head with a nailset.

"Penny" (abbreviated as "d") indicates a nail's length. Here are some equivalents in inches: 2d = 1", 3d = 1¼", 4d = 1½", 6d = 2".

Screws. Not all screws are created equal. Many projects call for hardened bugle-head *drywall* screws, now widely available as "multipurpose" screws. These versatile fasteners are an improvement over traditional woodscrews. If you substitute woodscrews, choose the next larger gauge number (diameter) in each case.

For a decorative touch, turn to *brass flathead* woodscrews with finishing washers. The heavy-duty *lag* screw is used with a flat washer and should be driven with a ratchet and socket.

Bolts. The *machine* bolt's square or hexagonal head is driven with a ratchet. *Carriage* bolts have self-anchoring heads that dig into wood as you tighten the nut.

To complement your bolts, use the standard "hex" nuts, T-nuts, wing nuts, or nylon-insert locknuts as specified.

Machine bolts need a flat washer at each end; carriage bolts require only one washer, inside the nut.

Adhesives. Adhesives vary according to strength, resistance to heat and water, and setting time.

Yellow (aliphatic resin) glue, often labeled "carpenter's glue" or "wood glue," is a good all-purpose adhesive. Though similar to white household glue, yellow glue has a higher resistance to heat, sets up faster, and is stronger.

Attach plastic laminate to wood surfaces with *contact cement.* It bonds immediately and needs no clamps. The older type of contact cement is highly flammable; buy the newer, water-base type if you can.

To position patterns and stencils, use artist's *spray-mount;* it's readily available in aerosol cans from art and hobby stores.

Fasteners for furniture

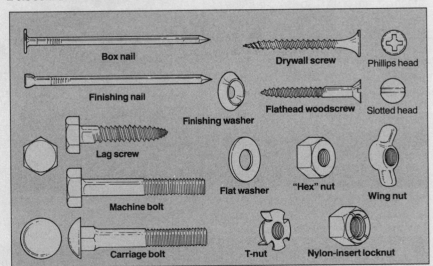

Box nail
Drywall screw
Phillips head
Finishing nail
Finishing washer
Flathead woodscrew
Slotted head
Lag screw
Flat washer
"Hex" nut
Wing nut
Machine bolt
Carriage bolt
T-nut
Nylon-insert locknut

Choose fasteners for your projects from this collection of nails, screws, and bolts.

Play kitchen

Transform a corner of your child's room into a scaled-down kitchen. Sized for children, this kitchen set includes a range with a peekaboo door, a sink cabinet with a plastic sink, and a refrigerator with shelves.

Each piece is actually a cabinet. All three are constructed in the same way, except for the mounting of the doors. The cabinets are made from ½-inch birch plywood with ¼-inch hardboard backs.

1. Cut all plywood pieces to size. Lay out backs **D** and **E** on the hardboard sheet and cut them to size.

Using a saber saw, make the cutout in one cabinet top **C** for the sink tub, making sure the hole is dimensioned to hold the tub securely. Also make the cutout in oven door **G** for the "window."

2. Assemble each cabinet with glue and nails, spacing nails 2 to 3 inches apart. Attach sides **A** or **B** to top **C**; attach bottom shelf **C** so its top surface is 2 inches up from the bottom of **A**. Add intermediate shelf **C** (two shelves for the refrigerator) and back **D** or **E**. Attach toekick **F**. Hang door **G** or **H** as shown in the large drawing, using a continuous hinge cut to fit (see Detail 1). Trim the range door slightly for a good fit.

3. Set the nails, fill the holes, and sand all surfaces. Apply a base coat of paint, then sand and dust well. Apply a top coat. When it's dry, paint circles on the rangetop with black enamel.

4. Screw on the door pulls and magnetic catches. Drop the tub in place.

Design: Don Vandervort.

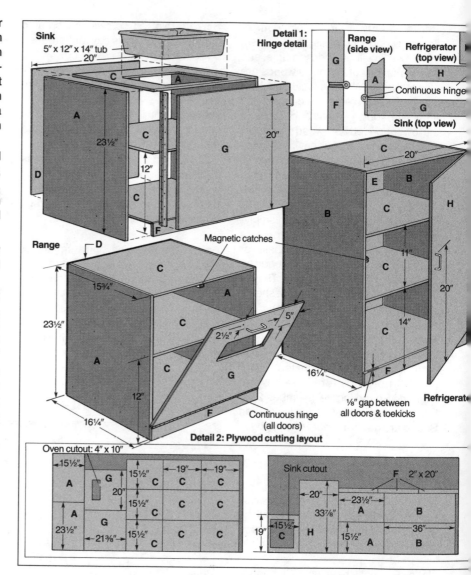

BUY		TO MAKE
Birch plywood (shop grade)		
2	½-inch 4 by 8-foot sheets	Pieces **A–C** and **F–H** (see plywood cutting layout)
Hardboard		
1	¼-inch 4 by 4-foot sheet	2 Backs **D**: ¼" by 20" by 23½"
		1 Back **E**: ¼" by 20" by 36"

MISCELLANEOUS

3d finishing nails • 2 continuous hinges, one 1 1⁄16" by 36" and one 1 1⁄16" by 48", with ½" screws
3 magnetic catches • Plastic sink tub, 5" by 12" by 14"
3 cabinet pulls • Wood glue • Wood putty • Nontoxic enamel

Both the doll house cabinets and the play kitchen components start from simple plywood boxes. The sink, range, and refrigerator, largely unadorned except for paint, can be built in a day. The town and country houses, dressed in 1/12-scale finery, are a bit more involved, yet each is an easy weekend project.

Doll house cabinets

Here's a pair of doll houses that your child won't outgrow: each sturdy house doubles as a roomy storage cabinet. Shown are two versions of the same basic structure—one a charming country cottage, the other a sophisticated town house (see the photo on page 19). Each is realistic without being time-consuming to build; construction is easy.

Both houses permit great freedom of decoration—let your imagination be your guide. Though each uses materials available at doll house specialty shops, you can fashion the decorative details from bits of standard molding or workshop scrap. Only basic tools are required, though a table saw is helpful for cutting the plywood.

1. For either house, cut all pieces to size.

2. Glue and nail all joints, spacing the nails 2 to 3 inches apart. Assemble sides **A**, floors **B**, and back **C**; mount front **C** with a continuous hinge (for the country house, cut the hinge down to 21 inches). This completes the town house.

To complete the country house, glue **E1** to **E2**, letting **E2** overlap; then glue and nail the pieces to the back. Nail through **E1** and **E2** into sides **A**; glue reinforcing pieces **F** in position as shown. Add four spacers **G**, trimming the hinge-side piece for door clearance.

3. To decorate the completed structure, take it to a doll house specialty shop or a hobby shop and experiment with the various items you'll find there: scale doors and windows, siding, shingles, fancy trim, and the like. Or decorate your house with pieces of standard molding.

Once you've chosen your materials, unscrew front **C**, and mark and cut openings for doors and windows. Size the openings to the manufacturer's specifications or, if you're building from scratch, size them to a scale of one inch per foot.

Prefinish the roof, walls, and trim, then glue the trim in place. To finish the country house as shown, whittle, finish, and attach half-timbering; then "plaster" the plywood with all-purpose patching compound, texturing by hand and with a whisk broom or stiff brush. Paint the shingles after attaching; paint the "plaster" when it's dry. Paint the interior, then glue walls **D** where desired. Reattach front **C**; add the catch.

Design: Scott Fitzgerrell.

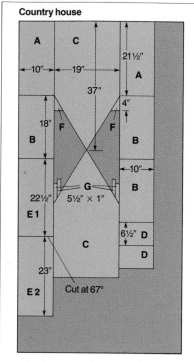

Detail: Plywood cutting layout

Country house

A C A

10″ 19″ 21½″

37″ 4″

18″ F F

B B

10″

22½″ G 5½″ × 1″ B

E1

6½″ D

C D

23″

E2 Cut at 67°

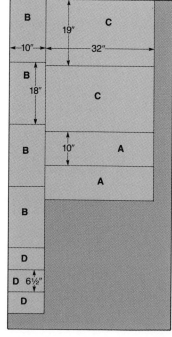

Town house

B C

10″ 19″ 32″

B

18″ C

B A

10″

A

B

D

D 6½″

D

BUY	TO MAKE
Fir plywood (grade AB)	
1 ½-inch 4 by 8-foot sheet	Pieces **A**–**G** for country house or pieces **A**–**D** for town house (see plywood cutting layout)

MISCELLANEOUS

1 continuous hinge, 1¹⁄₁₆″ by 30″, with ½″ screws • Magnetic catch • 2d finishing nails
Wood glue • Trim and finish (see below)

TRIM & FINISH

Country house: 550 sq. in. fish-scale shingle strips • 4′ of 1″ half-round molding for rakes
Ready-made windows • Ready-made door trim • All-purpose patching compound
15′ of ¼″ by 1½″ pine for half-timbering, door, chimney, and chimney pots
Ivory and slate gray enamel • Medium oak stain • Scale brick paper
Town house: 8′ of ¼″ by 1½″ pine for parapet, step, and curb
30″ of scale dentil cornice molding • Ready-made windows and door with classical trim
60″ of scale decorative band molding • 128″ of scale dentil molding for quoins
Navajo white spray enamel • Scale brick paper

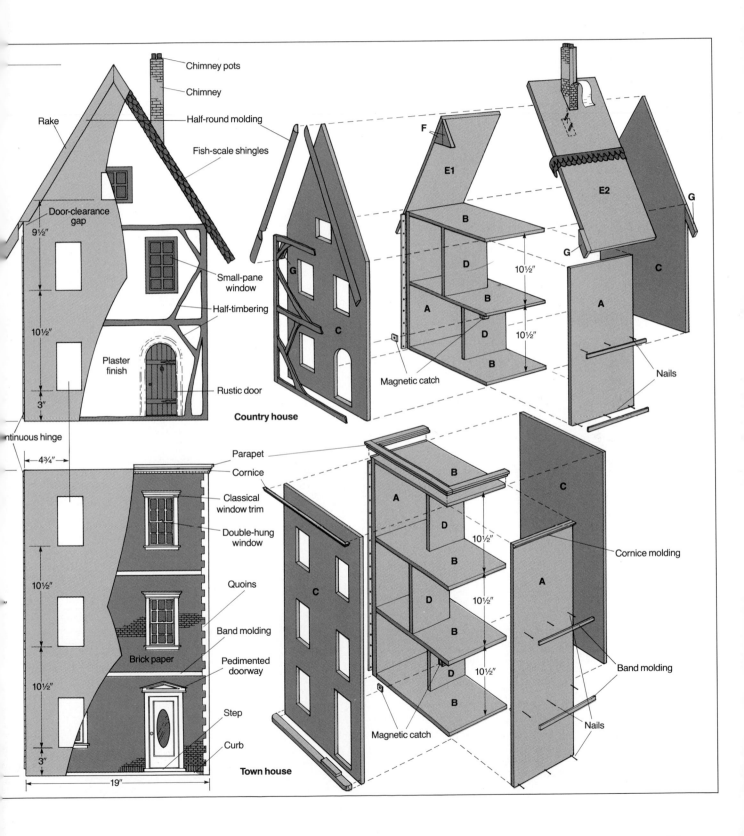

Chimney pots

Chimney

Half-round molding

Fish-scale shingles

Rake

Door-clearance gap

9½″

Small-pane window

Half-timbering

10½″

Plaster finish

Rustic door

3″

ntinuous hinge

Country house

G

C

F

E1

E2

G

G

B

D

B

A

D

B

10½″

10½″

Magnetic catch

C

A

Nails

4¾″

Parapet

Cornice

Classical window trim

Double-hung window

10½″

Quoins

Band molding

Brick paper

Pedimented doorway

10½″

Step

Curb

3″

19″

Town house

B

A

D

B

D

B

D

B

10½″

10½″

10½″

C

Magnetic catch

C

A

Cornice molding

Band molding

Nails

A capacious cargo hauler, the bright, bold van toybox on the left is easy to build and can be decorated to suit your fancy. On the right is the wooden wagon, an elegant, solid-oak heirloom designed to last for generations.

Custom van toybox

Building this plywood van—by yourself or with a child—is just part of the fun. Its expansive, flat sides offer great opportunities for custom decoration. And its ample capacity ensures its usefulness when cleanup time rolls around.

1. Lay out and cut sides **A**, back **B**, bottom **C**, and front **D** (see Detail 1). Lay out windshield **E** and cut to length only. Cut the molding into two fillers **G** and two bumpers **H** as shown. Cut axles **I** and mark center lines for them on **C**, 4 inches from each end.

2. Glue and nail the axles to the bottom, then add **A**, **B**, and **D**. Glue the fillers in place as shown.

3. Cut one long edge of windshield **E** at a 75° angle as shown. Hold it in position against **D**, mark its width, then cut the other long edge at a 75° angle. Glue and nail it in place.

4. Measure the top of the van and cut lid **F** in one piece. Cut the front edge at a 75° angle and cut the 3-inch hole as shown; then saw the piece in half. Cut the continuous hinge in half. Center it on each side and use it to attach the lids. Add weatherstripping where shown in the photo (this protects little fingers from being pinched). Attach the friction lid supports (use the manufacturer's instructions and the photo as guides; the lids should open just past vertical).

5. Round over all edges, set the nails, and fill the holes; then paint. Paint the windows and grille, following the layout in Detail 2. Finish bumpers **H** and attach. Trim the van as desired. We used automotive striping tape and vinyl letters from a stationery store. A word of caution: These materials can be peeled off and possibly ingested. An alternative is to use nontoxic paint for the trim. Finally, drill ⅜-inch pilot holes in the axles and add the wheels as shown.

Design: Bill Oetinger.

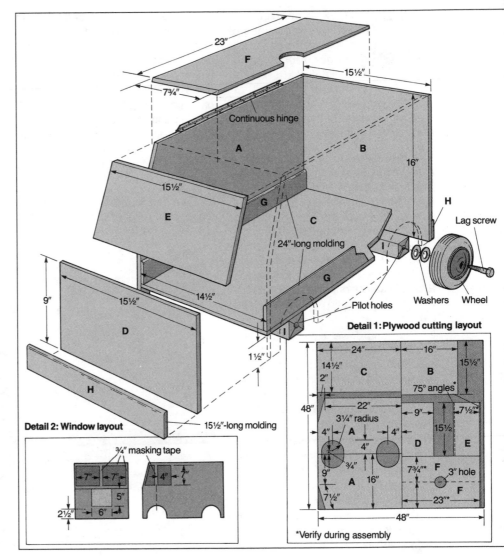

BUY		TO MAKE
Douglas fir plywood (grade AB)		
1	½-inch 4 by 4-foot sheet	Parts **A–F** (see Detail 1)
Clear pine, fir, or other softwood		
1	3-foot 2 by 2	2 Axles **I**: 1½″ by 1½″ by 14½″

MISCELLANEOUS
8′ of ⅜″ by 2¼″ pine molding • 1 continuous hinge, 1¹⁄₁₆″ by 30″, with ½″ screws
2 friction lid supports • Vinyl weatherstripping, ⅜″ by 8′
4 wheels, 1½″ by 6″ in diameter with a ½″ hub • 4 lag screws, ½″ by 3″, with 2 washers each
3d finishing nails • Wood glue • Wood putty • Nontoxic paint
Striping tape and vinyl letters (optional)

Heirloom wooden wagon

Oak construction makes this classic wagon as rugged as it is good-looking. To build it, you'll need a moderate level of woodworking skill, a radial-arm or table saw with a dado blade, and components for the steamer (see Detail 1).

1. Cut all pieces to size. Rabbet sides **A** and dado sides **A** and ends **B**. Use Detail 3 to locate and mark half-lap joints between yoke top **N** and yoke extensions **P**; cut the joints to fit (see large drawing). Rabbet the ends of **N**. Cut profiles and drill axle holes in axle supports **L** and **O** (see Details 5 and 6). Shape the ends of yoke extensions **P** (see Detail 3); drill ¼-inch bolt holes. Cut the dowel into twelve 1½-inch pieces.

2. Glue and dowel sides **A** and one end **B** (use three dowels per joint). Slip in bottom **C**; add remaining end **B**. Using glue and brads, fasten spacer blocks **D** and **E** (see large drawing and Detail 3). Glue stake supports **F** and **G** to the blocks.

3. To make each stake section, glue and screw together four stakes **H** and two stake connectors **I** as shown; countersink the screws and slightly bevel the lower ends of the stakes.

4. Glue and screw crosspiece **J** to support **K**; add axle supports **L** (see large drawing and Detail 5). Glue and screw support **M** to the underside of bottom **C** where shown in Detail 3 (**M** corresponds to the position of the front undercarriage). Center and drill a ⅛-inch hole through **M** and **C** and use as a guide to counterbore and drill **C** and **M** for the machine screw. Add the roller glides (see Detail 3).

Glue and screw yoke top **N** to axle supports **O** and yoke extensions **P**; add crosspiece **Q**. Drill a ⁵⁄₁₆-inch hole in the center of **N**. Cut and screw an aluminum angle along each inside edge of **P** and trim flush at the ends.

5. Nail together and cut bending form halves **R** (see Detail 1). Make the steamer as shown, pour in about a quart of water, and bring to a boil. Add pieces **S**, cover, and steam for about 4 hours or until pliable (check water supply periodically). Put the pieces in the form as shown, making sure the long edges are flush. Tightly clamp and leave overnight. Release, apply glue to all mating surfaces, and reclamp; leave overnight.

6. Glue handle pieces **T** and **U** to the tongue (see Detail 2). Shape as shown.

Trim and round over the other end of the tongue; drill the ¼-inch bolt hole. Plug all visible screws, round over sharp edges, sand, and apply two finish coats.

7. Drill four counterbore holes in bottom **C** for the carriage bolts (see Detail 3); attach the rear undercarriage. Attach the front undercarriage (see Detail 4) and the tongue. Cut axles to length from the rods and install; mount the wheels as shown and attach the axle caps. Add the rubber mat and the stake sides.

Design: Don Vandervort.

BUY		TO MAKE		
Oak (grade to suit)				
9	board feet of 4/4 stock	2	Sides **A**:	¹³⁄₁₆″ by 5″ by 36″
		2	Ends **B**:	¹³⁄₁₆″ by 5″ by 17⅛″
		2	Rear axle supports **L**:	¹³⁄₁₆″ by 5″ by 12⅛″
		1	Rear support **K**:	¹³⁄₁₆″ by 5″ by 12⅜″
		1	Rear crosspiece **J**:	¹³⁄₁₆″ by 5″ by 12⅜″
		1	Front support **M**:	¹³⁄₁₆″ by 5″ by 14″
		1	Yoke top **N**:	¹³⁄₁₆″ by 5″ by 14″
		2	Front axle supports **O**:	¹³⁄₁₆″ by 5″ by 7½″
		2	Yoke extensions **P**:	¹³⁄₁₆″ by 2″ by 15″
		1	Front crosspiece **Q**:	¹³⁄₁₆″ by 2½″ by 12⅜″
Oak flooring				
6	⁵⁄₁₆-inch by 2-inch by 12-foot pieces	8	Spacer blocks **D**:	⁵⁄₁₆″ by 2″ by 1¹⁵⁄₁₆″
		2	Spacer blocks **E**:	⁵⁄₁₆″ by 2″ by 4½″
		2	Stake supports **F**:	⁵⁄₁₆″ by 2″ by 36⅝″
		2	Stake supports **G**:	⁵⁄₁₆″ by 2″ by 19¼″
		24	Stakes **H**:	⁵⁄₁₆″ by 2″ by 16″
		12	Stake connectors **I**:	⁵⁄₁₆″ by 2″ by 14″
		3	Tongue pieces **S**:	⁵⁄₁₆″ by 1¾″ by 29½″
		2	Handle pieces **T**:	⁵⁄₁₆″ by 1¾″ by 8¼″
		2	Handle pieces **U**:	⁵⁄₁₆″ by 1¾″ by 3¼″
Douglas fir (construction grade)				
1	6-foot 2 by 6	2	Bending form halves **R**:	1½″ by 5½″ by 36″
Fir plywood (grade AD)				
1	⅝-inch 2 by 3-foot piece	1	Bottom **C**:	⅝″ by 17⅛″ by 35⅛″

MISCELLANEOUS

2′ of ⅜″ hardwood dowel • 2 pieces of aluminum angle, each ¾″ by ¾″ by 10″
4 roller glides, ¾″ in diameter • 2 galvanized steel rods, each ½″ by 18″ • 8 ½″ washers
4 wheels, 10″ in diameter, with ½″ hubs • 4 knock-on axle caps, ½″ in diameter
96 brass flathead woodscrews, ½″ by #6 • 10 flathead woodscrews, ¾″ by #6
28 drywall screws, 1¼″ by #6 • Brads • 4 carriage bolts, ¼″ by 1½″, with nuts and washers
1 machine bolt, ¼″ by 4″, with locknut and 2 washers
1 machine screw, ⁵⁄₁₆″ by 3½″, with 2 locknuts and 2 washers
Wood glue • Wood putty • Clear penetrating oil finish • Black rubber mat, 34⅜″ by 16⅜″

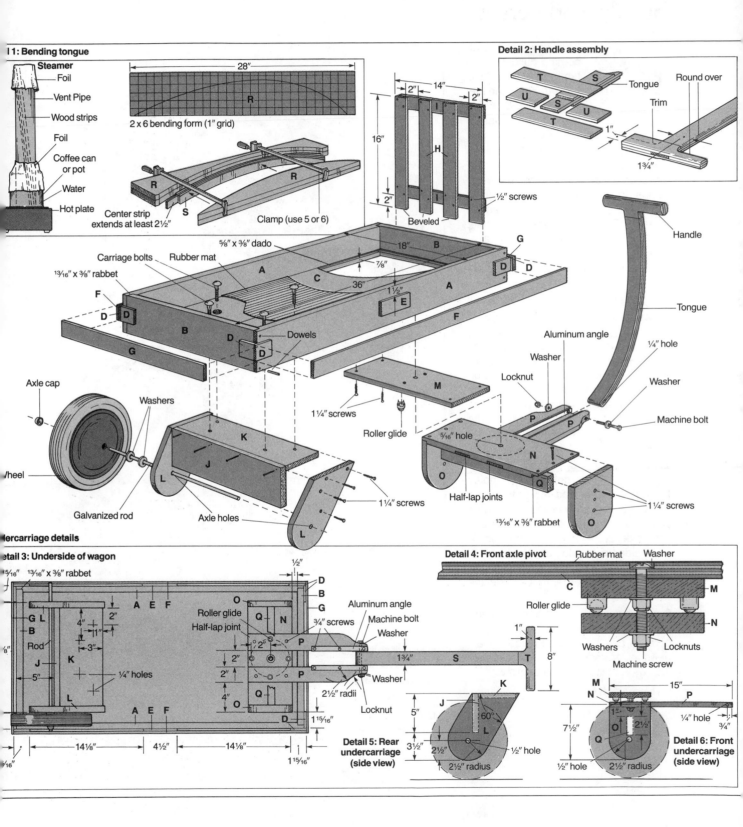

Sturdy workbench

If you have an up-and-coming builder in the family, this project is for you. You'll find that a small investment in time and materials is repaid many times over by a workbench that's rigid, durable, and versatile.

Key features include simple construction, a replaceable top that overhangs its base for easy mounting of vises and clamps, and a convenient tool rack. The design is also adaptable: you can vary the length of the detachable legs to suit the user, or scale up the entire structure if you wish—right up to adult size.

1. Cut all pieces to size (see detail drawing). Glue and screw ends **B** to sides **A**, good sides out, as shown. Check the frame as the glue dries to be sure it's square. Then add one top **C**, aligning it flush with the edge of **A** on the tool-holder side as shown. (The top overhangs the other three sides by 1½ inches.) Fasten **C** to the frame with glue and 10 screws. Countersink the screws.

2. With the unit upside down, clamp legs **F** in place, drill ⁵⁄₁₆-inch holes through sides **A** and the legs where shown, and fasten each leg to the frame with two carriage bolts. Turn the unit right side up. Add the second top **C**, good side up, but do not glue; instead, attach it with 10 screws spaced a little inside those underneath. Countersink the screws.

3. Screw spacer **D** in place, then add tool rack **E**, fastening it with paired screws. Don't glue **E** in place—you'll need to remove it to change to longer legs as your little carpenter grows.

Design: Scott Fitzgerrell.

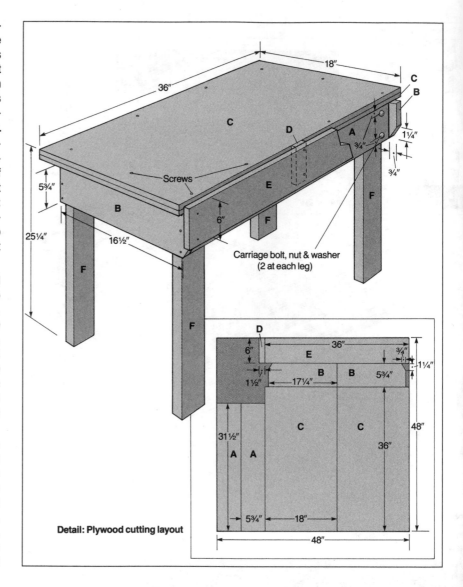

Detail: Plywood cutting layout

BUY		TO MAKE	
Douglas fir plywood (grade AD)			
1	¾-inch 4 by 4-foot sheet	Parts **A–E** (see detail drawing)	
Standard and better fir			
1	8-foot 2 by 4	4 Legs **F**: 1½" by 3½" by 23¾"*	

MISCELLANEOUS

8 carriage bolts, ⁵⁄₁₆" by 2½", with nuts and washers
40 drywall screws, 1¼" by #6 • Wood glue

*Cut the legs shorter if desired; for longer legs, use a 10 or 12-foot 2 by 4 instead.

A half-sheet of plywood, a 2 by 4, basic tools, and an hour of time are about all it takes to build this solid little workbench. Young carpenters will appreciate its scaled-down proportions—and it's a simple matter to raise the height of the bench as the carpenter grows.

TOOLS OF THE TRADE

What tools do you need to build the projects in this book? Among the basics are a tape measure, try or combination square, compass, crosscut saw, electric drill and twist bits, hammer, screwdriver, adjustable wrench, vise, and C-clamps. Two standard carpentry tools, a carpenter's square and chalkline, will help you lay out cutting lines or grids when a try or combination square is too small.

Today's woodworkers also consider the following tools basic:

Portable circular saw. Using a circular saw and the correct blade, you can cut faster and more accurately than with a handsaw. The popular 7¼-inch model cuts through surfaced 2-by lumber at any angle from 45° to 90°. Combination and plywood blades handle basic cutting chores.

Portable saber saw. This easy-to-use saw specializes in curves and cutouts. The variable-speed models allow fine control when cutting tight curves or different types of wood. Look for a saw with a tilting baseplate for cutting bevels to a 45° angle. Stock up on blades for rough cutting and tight curves.

Table and radial-arm saws. Real time-savers when you're doing a lot of cutting, these stationary machines can handle such precision cuts as rabbets and dadoes. The 10-inch models can crosscut 4-by lumber.

A table saw, a circular saw that's permanently mounted in a table, has locking rip fences and miter gauges that make it the saw of choice for crosscutting short lengths of wood or for ripping.

A radial-arm saw is mounted on an arm above the table and drawn across the material. You can raise, lower, tilt, and even swivel the saw for miter cuts or narrow rip cuts. Though you can crosscut long pieces with ease, ripping—or even crosscutting—large sheets is difficult.

Miter box. If you're cutting trim or narrow stock with a handsaw, use a miter box to guide the saw at a fixed 45° or 90° angle.

The woodworker's tool kit

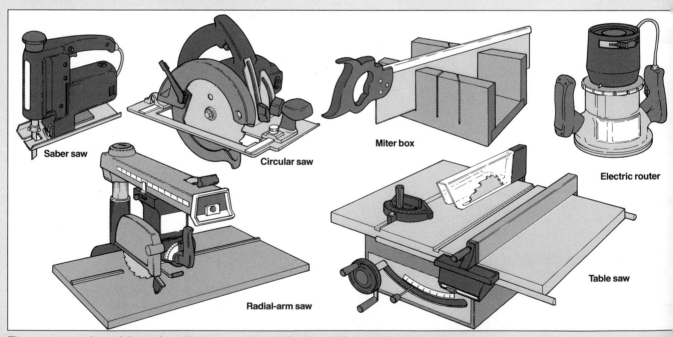

Saber saw · Circular saw · Miter box · Electric router · Radial-arm saw · Table saw

These power and specialty tools make clean, quick work of cutting, drilling, and finishing.

Electric router. A router equipped with the proper bit makes short work of dadoes, rabbets, and other grooves; it will also round or bevel the edges of a board and trim plastic laminate in a single pass. Straight, rabbeting, rounding-over, chamfer, cove, core-box, and laminate-trimming bits are the ones used in the projects.

Butt chisel. A sharp butt chisel helps pare notches, smooth the bottoms of grooves, and square rounded edges. A ¾-inch-wide blade is a good general-purpose size.

Jack plane. To smooth and square-up board faces and sides, choose a 14-inch-long jack plane.

Four-in-hand. Files and rasps shape and smooth wood to its final form. The four-in-hand has file and rasp teeth on both sides of its half-round profile.

Electric drill bits. The following bits produce larger holes and cleaner results than twist bits:

- *Spade bits* are the standard for holes from ⅜ to 1½ inches in diameter.
- *Brad point bits* (¼ to 1 inch) are preferred when appearance counts.
- *Hole saws* bore holes up to 4 inches in diameter.
- *Pilot bits* drill countersink and counterbore holes simultaneously.
- *Standard* and *Phillips screwdriver bits* drive screws effortlessly.

Spring and pipe clamps. Spring clamps excel at fixing guides for sawing. Buy a pair with at least 2-inch jaw capacity. For clamping tabletops and other wide assemblies, attach pipe clamps to any length of ½ or ¾-inch steel pipe that suits your job.

Ratchet and socket set. These are essential for tightening countersunk or counterbored bolts and lag screws. A ⅜-inch-drive ratchet and matching 12-point socket set is your best bet.

Belt and finishing sanders. Large belt sanders abrade wood quickly—they're best for shaping, rounding, and smoothing over large areas. For a finer finish, choose a finishing sander.

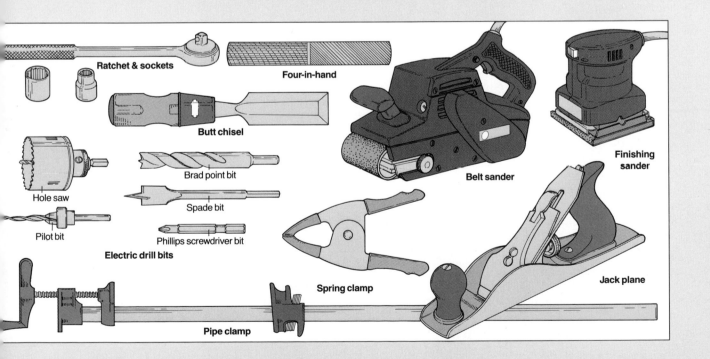

Ratchet & sockets

Four-in-hand

Butt chisel

Finishing sander

Hole saw

Brad point bit

Belt sander

Spade bit

Pilot bit

Phillips screwdriver bit

Electric drill bits

Spring clamp

Jack plane

Pipe clamp

The toddler is sitting on the fold-down stepstool. His bear buddy is trying the rocker side of the multiposition chair (the other chairs show two other positions). Both projects are easy to build.

Multiposition chair

This simple chair offers a small child a variety of options. Rotating it from one side to another changes it from a low rocker to a chair to a stepstool to a stool (see the illustrations below).

Construction is easy—simply cut out the parts, and glue and nail them together. You'll need only basic tools and a saber saw to build the chair.

You might also consider making several of the chairs at once. Since so little lumber is required for each chair, and since most suppliers sell the necessary 1 by 12s and 1 by 8s in minimum 6-foot lengths, you'll almost certainly have enough wood to build at least two. And because construction is so easy, a child can help you—perhaps in making one as a present for a friend or younger sibling.

1. Cut all pieces to size. Cut the curve along one long edge of each side **A** with a saber saw. (Note: The curve has a 35¾-inch radius. Use a yardstick tacked to a workbench to help you mark the arc.) Also cut the 86° angle at one end of each side **A** (see the detail drawing).

2. To make each hand-hold, drill a pair of 1-inch holes on 3-inch centers. Using a saber saw, cut from one hole to its mate.

3. Mark the placement of seat boards **B** on the sides where shown. Glue and nail the sides to one seat board, then to the other. Nail through the back of one board into the edge of the other as shown in the detail drawing, spacing nails every 3 inches.

4. Set the nails and fill the holes. Sand all surfaces, easing the edges, and finish.

Design: Don Vandervort.

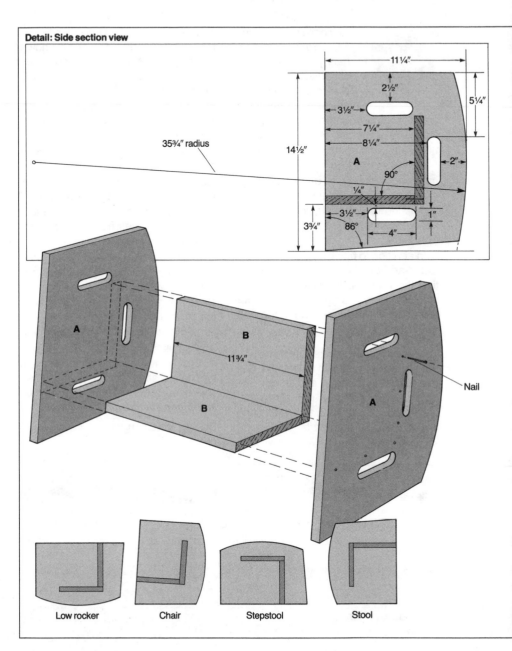

Detail: Side section view

35¾″ radius

11¼″
2½″
5¼″
3½″
7¼″
8¼″
14½″
A
2″
90°
¼″
3¾″
3½″
1″
86°
4″

11¾″

B

A

B

Nail

A

Low rocker   Chair   Stepstool   Stool

BUY		TO MAKE	
Clear pine			
1	3-foot 1 by 12	2 Sides **A**:	¾″ by 11¼″ by 14½″
1	2-foot 1 by 8	2 Seat boards **B**:	¾″ by 7¼″ by 11¾″

MISCELLANEOUS
5d finishing nails • Wood glue • Wood putty • Clear penetrating oil finish

Fold-down stepstool

Any child will appreciate the boost this handy little stepstool can give. It's invaluable for reaching such adult-height items as water faucets, countertops, and cookie jars. The stepstool, pictured on page 30, is also light enough for easy toting.

Construction (from pine or fir, and hardwood dowel) is quick, inexpensive, and strong. Take special care to cut accurately, though, for this is the key to the stepstool's strength and easy operation.

In addition to basic tools, you'll find a radial-arm or table saw helpful for cutting the rabbets. A router, which can also cut the rabbets, is useful for rounding over edges—an important detail for a project such as this.

1. Cut all pieces to size. Cut the handhold in top **B** as shown in Detail 3. Cut the profiles in sides **A** and **D**; cut rabbets in **A** and **D** and drill three flat-bottomed holes in each side **A** and one in each side **D** (see the large drawing

and Details 1 and 2). Drill holes for one brace **C** through sides **D** as shown. (Note: Sides **A** are paired and must mirror each other; likewise, sides **D**. Keep track of their proper orientation as you work.) Finally, mark all screw locations on sides **A** and **D** as shown, and drill countersink and pilot holes.

2. Assemble the pivoting step pieces **D**, **E**, and **F** with glue and screws. Putty the screw heads, then round over all edges; sand smooth. Fit one brace **C** through the holes in sides **D** and make sure that it rotates freely; if not, sand either the dowel or the holes.

3. Assemble the completed step, stool sides **A**, and remaining braces **C** with glue and screws as shown. Fit top **B** in place. Mark the position and angle of the rip cut on its forward edge (see large drawing). Cut the top and fasten it with glue and screws as shown.

4. Round over all remaining edges, fill the holes, sand carefully, and finish. (We used two coats of satin polyurethane for a durable, washable surface.)

Design: Bill Oetinger.

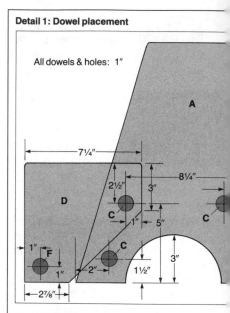

Detail 1: Dowel placement

All dowels & holes: 1"

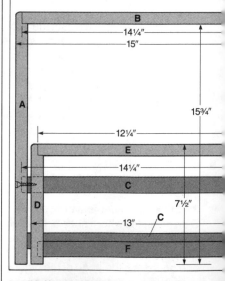

Detail 2: Front elevation

BUY		TO MAKE
Clear pine or fir		
1	3-foot 1 by 12	2 Stool sides **A**: ¾" by 11¼" by 15¾"
1	4-foot 1 by 8	1 Stool top **B**: ¾" by 7¼" by 14¼"
		2 Step sides **D**: ¾" by 7¼" by 7½"
		1 Step top **E**: ¾" by 7¼" by 12¼"
Hardwood dowel		
1	5-foot or 2 3-foot 1-inch-diameter pieces	3 Braces **C**: 1" by 14¼"
		1 Brace **F**: 1" by 12¼"

MISCELLANEOUS
24 drywall screws, 1¼" by #6 • Wood glue • Wood putty • Clear nontoxic finish

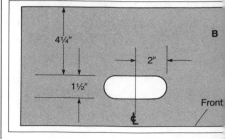

Detail 3: Hand-hold layout

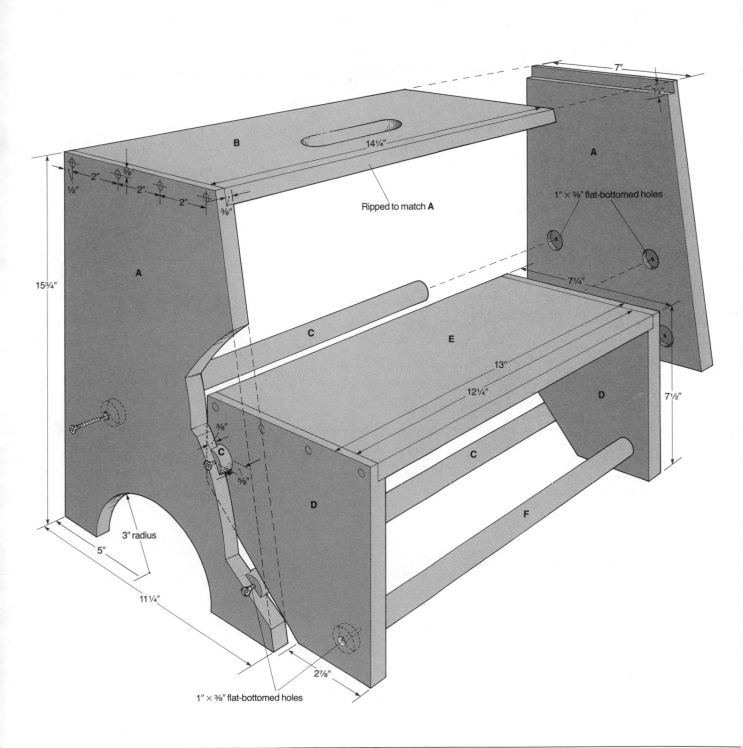

B

A

14¼"

Ripped to match **A**

7"

¾"

A

1" × ⅜" flat-bottomed holes

½"

2"

⅜"

2"

⅜"

2"

15¾"

A

7¼"

C

E

7½"

13"

12¼"

D

C

⅜"

C

⅝"

D

C

D

F

3" radius

5"

11¼"

2⅞"

1" × ⅜" flat-bottomed holes

Chair menagerie

Here's a happy collection of animals guaranteed to capture any child's imagination. You can build this set of chairs with just basic tools and a saber saw. You'll need a steady hand for the paint job, but the patterns are simple and even beginners should get good results.

1. Cut all pieces to size (to transfer grid patterns, see page 36). Cut finger holes in seat backs **E** and drill countersink and pilot holes in cleats **D** and **F** (see Detail 1). Round over all exposed edges, either by hand or with a router and ½-inch rounding-over bit set ⅜ inch high. Putty all plywood edges and sand all parts.

2. Glue and nail elements **B** to profiles **A**, cleats **D** to seats **C**, and cleats **F** to seat backs **E**. Set the nails and fill the holes; then sand.

3. Screw (do not glue) the seats and backs to profiles **A** without drilling pilot holes in **A** (set the seat height to suit your child, but stay within the seat-mounting area indicated on each plan). For the nonrocking chairs, keep the seats level and the backs angled as shown in Detail 1. On the swan rocker, angle the backward-facing seat 5° to 10° and attach the back at a 90° angle to the seat. To guard against tipping over backward, fasten the seat back as close to the rear edge of the swan's neck as possible.

4. With the chairs assembled, paint the background color on all surfaces. Let the paint dry; then disassemble the chairs. Paint the designs as shown, either freehand or using a paper stencil attached with spray mounting adhesive—let the adhesive dry before applying the stencil. After the paint dries, reassemble the chairs, this time using glue as well as screws.

Design: Sandra Popovich & Scott Fitzgerrell.

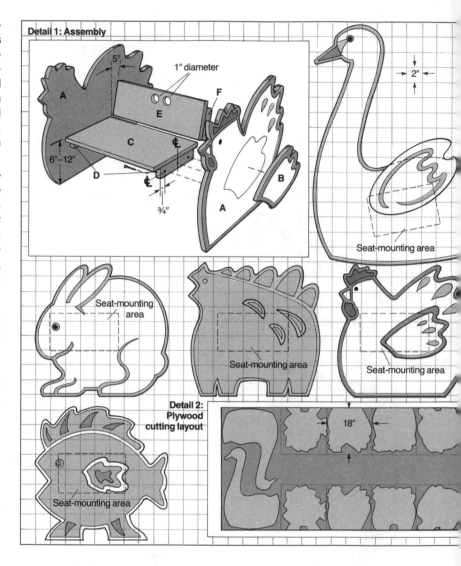

BUY		TO MAKE	
Birch plywood (shop grade)			
1	¾-inch 4 by 8-foot sheet	10	Animal profiles **A** (see Detail 2)
			Applied elements **B** (cut from scrap)
Pine or fir			
1	6-foot 1 by 10	5	Seats **C**: ¾" by 9¼" by 12"
1	6-foot 1 by 6	5	Seat backs **E**: ¾" by 5½" by 12"
1	10-foot 1 by 2	10	Cleats **D**: ¾" by 1½" by 8"
		10	Cleats **F**: ¾" by 1½" by 3¾"
MISCELLANEOUS			
4d nails • 50 drywall screws, 1¼" by #6 • Wood glue • Wood putty • Nontoxic enamel			

Fish, fowl, swan, bunny, or dinosaur—it's hard to choose a seat from such an appealing group. You can mix or match designs and adjust seat heights to fit the child.

MARKING, CUTTING & DRILLING

Marking, cutting, and drilling are fundamental to virtually every woodworking project. Here are some tips to help you achieve clean, accurate results the first time around.

Caution: Whenever you use power tools, be sure to wear safety goggles.

Layout techniques

For most layout tasks, you need only a tape measure, combination square, and pencil. Add more specialized tools—such as a carpenter's square, chalkline, or compass—as you need them.

One note: The symbol ₵, used on some project drawings, indicates the center line of the element shown.

Marking straight lines. When measuring cutting lines on solid lumber, lay the tape along the edge of the material and always pull the tape taut against the end hook. Mark the distance, then draw the line with the help of a try or combination square (make sure the thickness of the line lies on the waste side of the material).

Measure and mark wide sheet materials at several points, then connect the marks with a carpenter's square or chalkline. To use a chalkline, pull out the cord and stretch it between the end marks. Then, holding the chalkline toward one end, lift it and release quickly so it snaps down sharply.

If you're cutting out several identical components, mark and cut the first, check it, then use it as a pattern to trace each additional piece.

Marking circles and arcs. A simple compass draws limited circles and arcs; wing dividers, available in larger sizes, are more precise. For large curves and circles, make a beam compass: tack one end of a thin board or yardstick to the material, hold a pencil at the desired radius, and pivot.

Transferring grids. To transfer gridded patterns, mark the edges of the material at the scale indicated in the plan and connect the marks with straight lines. Mark the intersections of a curving line from square to square, then connect the marks with freehand lines, or use a French or flexible curve (available in art or drafting supply stores).

For clean cuts

The number of teeth per inch along a saw blade determines the kind of cut it makes. The more teeth, the smoother —but slower—the cut. To hide the splintering that occurs where saw teeth

Three techniques for clean cutting

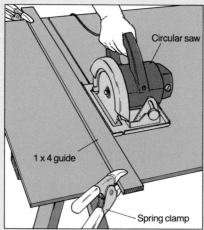

For long, straight cuts, clamp a scrap guide to the material and let the saw ride against it.

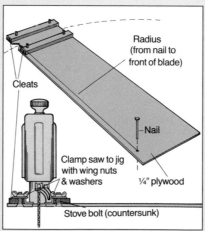

Cut large arcs and circles with a saber saw and jig. Adapt the basic design to fit your saw's baseplate.

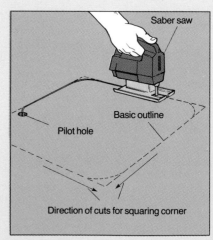

To make rectangular cutouts, drill a pilot hole for the saw's blade, cut the basic outline, then square each corner.

exit, cut with the good side *up* when using a handsaw, table saw, or when crosscutting with a radial-arm saw; if you're using a portable circular saw or saber saw, or ripping with a radial-arm saw, cut with the good side *down*.

Sawing straight lines. The key to sawing straight is using a guide. If your saw doesn't have one, improvise a guide from a *straight* length of scrap lumber and two clamps, as shown on the facing page. Cushion the jaws of the clamp to protect the work. Be sure to allow for the thickness of the blade—or "kerf"—when cutting; otherwise, the finished piece will be too short.

Sawing curves, circles, and cutouts. Arcs, curves, and circles are all jobs for a saber saw. When cutting curves, use the finest blade you can. The tighter the curve, the more slowly you should cut.

You can execute a circle with a radius up to 6 or 7 inches with the help of a circle guide. To cut larger arcs and circles, such as the rockers for the projects on pages 6–9 and the wheels for the wagon bed on pages 78–81, try building your own saber saw jig from a straight board or plywood strip, pivoting pin (such as a nail), and some type of sturdy attachment between the jig and baseplate (see facing page).

For cutouts inside a panel, first drill a pilot hole in the waste area for the saber saw blade, as shown on the facing page. Cut the basic outline. If the corners must be square, round them off on the first pass, then finish by sawing into the corners. If they must be tightly curved, first drill the arcs with an electric drill and brad point bit or hole saw (see page 29).

Drilling tips

Be sure to clamp down small materials before drilling. If possible, match the drill speed to the job: highest speeds for small bits and softwoods, slowest speeds for large bits and hardwoods. When drilling large holes in tough materials, first make a small lead hole.

Drilling pilot holes. Screws require predrilled pilot holes in all but the softest materials. For *drywall screws,* use a ³⁄₃₂-inch bit for #6 screws, a ¹⁄₈-inch bit for #8 screws. In softwoods, drill half as deep as the screw's length, two-thirds to three-quarters the length in hardwoods. For *woodscrews,* pick a drill bit the diameter of the screw's unthreaded shank and drill as deep as the shank's length.

Flathead screws are typically countersunk to sit flush or just below the surface; often, they're counterbored, then covered with putty or a wood plug (see below). To drill these holes, choose either a second bit (⁵⁄₁₆-inch for #6 drywall screws, ³⁄₈-inch for #8) or a special pilot bit (see page 29).

Solving drilling problems. To drill straight holes in a board's face, use a portable drill stand; a doweling jig works well along edges (see below). Or drill a scrap block and then use the block for a guide.

To keep the back side of the wood from breaking away, lay or clamp a wood scrap firmly against the back of your work and drill through the piece into the scrap.

To stop a drill bit at a specified depth, use a pilot bit, wrap electrical or masking tape around the bit at the correct depth, or buy a stop collar specially designed for the purpose.

Pilot hole profiles

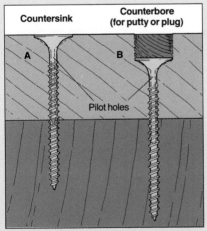

Drilling screw holes: Countersink hole (A) lets the screw sit at or just below the surface; counterbore hole (B) hides screw.

Guides for drilling

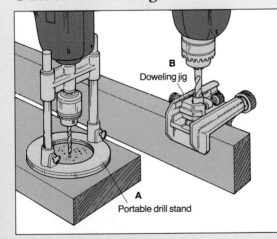

To keep a drill bit moving in the right path, use a portable drill stand (A) or a doweling jig (B).

Modular design is the key to these two storage systems: each is basically two large cabinets connected by smaller cabinets or shelves. The closet organizer at left can be customized to fit available closet space. The modular wall unit at right can tame the most unruly room.

Modular wall system

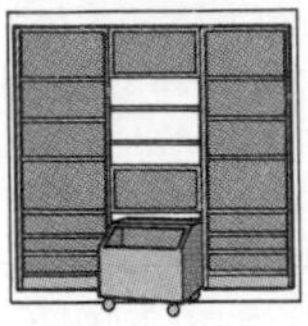

Order from chaos—that's what this modular wall system can create. The adjustable shelves and rolling cart store treasures, books, and toys neatly and accessibly.

The wall system is made of two tall cabinets joined by two small cabinets. Adjustable shelves between the cabinets, as well as inside them, offer plenty of flexible storage. The rolling cart, garaged between the two tall cabinets, provides handy storage for laundry or oversized toys.

Components are built from standard-dimension softwood and birch

BUY		TO MAKE		
Clear pine or Douglas fir				
1	4-foot 1 by 3	2	Toekicks **F**:	¾" by 2½" by 23¼"
4	6-foot 1 by 12s	4	Uprights **A**:	¾" by 11¼" by 72"
2	12-foot 1 by 12s	10	Fixed shelves **B**:	¾" by 11¼" by 24"
1	10-foot 1 by 12	4	Sides **C**:	¾" by 11¼" by 12¾"
		2	Adjustable shelves **H**:	¾" by 11¼" by 24½"
2	10-foot 1 by 12s	10	Adjustable shelves **G**:	¾" by 11¼" by 23"
Birch plywood (shop grade)				
1	¼-inch 4 by 8-foot sheet	Backs **D** and **E** (see Detail 1)		
1	¾-inch 4 by 4-foot sheet	Cart pieces **I–M** (see Detail 1)		

MISCELLANEOUS
48 shelf pegs • 4 1¾" plate-mounted casters with screws • 5d finishing nails
2d nails • 4 woodscrews, 2½" by #8
Wood glue • Wood putty • Clear penetrating oil finish
8 carriage bolts, ¼" by 1¼", with nuts and washers

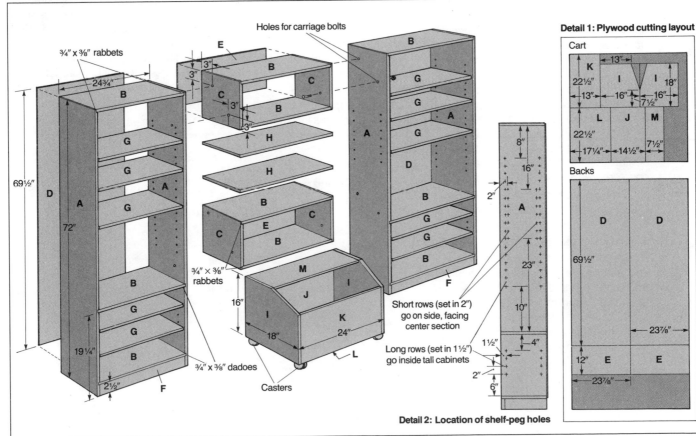

Holes for carriage bolts

¾" x ⅜" rabbets

Detail 1: Plywood cutting layout

Cart

Backs

¾" × ⅜" rabbets

¾" x ⅜" dadoes

Casters

Short rows (set in 2")
go on side, facing
center section

Long rows (set in 1½")
go inside tall cabinets

Detail 2: Location of shelf-peg holes

. . . Modular wall system

plywood. In addition to basic tools, you'll need a radial-arm or table saw for cutting rabbets and dadoes.

Refer to the drawings on page 39 as you work.

1. Cut all pieces to size (see Detail 1). Rabbet and dado uprights **A** and rabbet sides **C** where shown.

2. Label each upright **A** to remember its position. Mark for placement of shelf-peg holes (see Detail 2) and drill. (Note: The two center uprights are drilled on both sides. The holes on the inside of the cabinets are 1½ inches from the edges. The holes on the outside are spaced 2 inches from the edges so they're offset from the holes on the inside. The vertical spacing for all holes is 2 inches; the depth is ½ inch.)

3. To assemble the cabinets, glue and nail uprights **A** and sides **C** to fixed shelves **B** with 5d nails spaced 3 inches apart; set the nails. Letting backs **D** and **E** overlap the uprights ⁵⁄₁₆ inch and letting **E** overlap shelves **B** ⅜ inch, attach the backs with glue and 2d nails spaced 5 inches apart. Attach toekicks **F** with glue and 5d nails; set the nails. Drill counterbores and holes for carriage bolts in sides **C**, align with the center uprights, and mark and drill counterbores and holes in the uprights.

4. Glue and nail together cart pieces **I–M**, using 5d nails spaced 3 inches apart. Screw casters to the bottom.

5. Fill holes, sand, and finish.

6. Stand up the tall cabinets in place and bolt the small cabinets to them. Add shelf pegs and adjustable shelves **G** and **H**. Using two woodscrews for each, fasten the tall cabinets to wall studs through the top of the backs. Store the cart in the center section.

Design: Don Vandervort.

Closet organizer

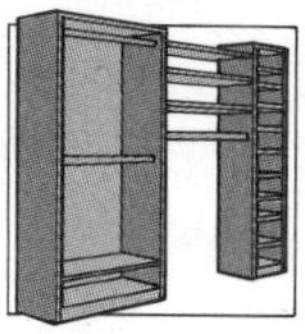

Standard closets waste space when used to store children's clothes. Blouses, shirts, and pants often hang out of a child's reach on the closet pole, leaving unused space below.

This closet organizer, pictured on page 38, is a simple adaptation of the modular wall system. It offers two levels of hanging space, the lower one easily reached by children. In addition, the organizer presents a column of shelves for shoes, sweaters, and such.

The unit shown is for a closet about 5 feet wide. For closets of other sizes, you can change the dimensions of the shelves and closet poles that connect the two cabinets—and even the cabinets themselves. (However, don't span more than 4 feet with the closet poles.)

1. Cut all lumber to size except center shelves **L** and closet poles **H** and **I**. Rabbet and dado uprights **A** where shown.

2. Label each upright **A** to remember its position; then mark for placement of the ½-inch-deep shelf-peg holes (as shown in the detail drawings) and drill. (Note: The two center uprights are drilled on both sides; the holes on the inside of the narrow cabinet are spaced 1½ inches from the edges so they're offset from those on the outside.)

3. To assemble the cabinets, glue and nail uprights **A** to fixed shelves **B** and **C** with 5d finishing nails; set the nails. Letting backs **J** and **K** overlap the uprights ⅜ inch, attach the backs with glue and 2d nails spaced 5 inches apart. Attach toekicks **F** and **G** with glue and 5d nails; set the nails.

4. Fill holes, sand, and finish.

5. Stand up the cabinets in the closet. Measure the distance between them and cut shelves **L** and closet poles **H** and **I** to fit, allowing for pole brackets and shelf pegs. Mount the brackets on the sides of the cabinets. Add closet poles **H** and **I**, shelf pegs, and adjustable shelves **D**, **E**, and **L**. Using two woodscrews for each, fasten the cabinets to wall studs through the top of the backs.

Design: Don Vandervort.

BUY		TO MAKE			
Clear pine or Douglas fir					
1	3-foot 1 by 3	1	Toekick	**F**:	¾″ by 2½″ by 23¼″
		1	Toekick	**G**:	¾″ by 2½″ by 11¼″
4	6-foot 1 by 12s	4	Uprights	**A**:	¾″ by 11¼″ by 72″
1	8-foot 1 by 12	2	Fixed shelves	**B**:	¾″ by 11¼″ by 24″
		2	Fixed shelves	**C**:	¾″ by 11¼″ by 12″
2	8-foot 1 by 12s	8	Adjustable shelves	**D**:	¾″ by 11¼″ by 10⅞″
		1	Adjustable shelf	**E**:	¾″ by 11¼″ by 22⅞″
		3	Adjustable shelves	**L**:	Cut to fit (up to 24″)
Closet pole round					
1	6-foot by 1⅜-inch diameter	2	Closet poles	**H**:	Cut to fit
		1	Closet pole	**I**:	Cut to fit (up to 24″)
Birch plywood (shop grade)					
1	¼-inch 4 by 8-foot sheet	1	Back	**J**:	¼″ by 24″ by 69½″
		1	Back	**K**:	¼″ by 12″ by 69½″

MISCELLANEOUS

3 pairs closet pole brackets • 48 shelf pegs • 5d finishing nails
2d nails • 4 woodscrews, 2½″ by #8
Wood glue • Wood putty • Clear penetrating oil finish

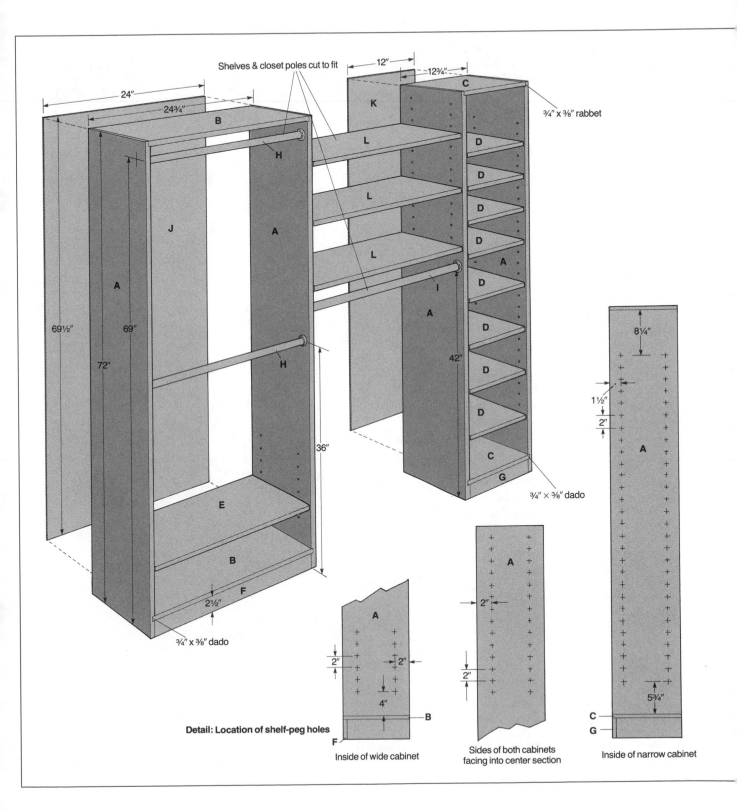

Shelves & closet poles cut to fit

24"

24¾"

B

H

12"

12¾"

K

C

¾" x ⅜" rabbet

L

D

L

D

D

J

A

L

D

A

A

D

A

A

D

H

D

D

69½"

69"

72"

42"

C

G

¾" × ⅜" dado

36"

E

B

F

2½"

¾" x ⅜" dado

8¼"

1½"

2"

A

A

A

2"

A

5¾"

2"

2"

4"

B

2"

F

C

G

Detail: Location of shelf-peg holes

Inside of wide cabinet

Sides of both cabinets
facing into center section

Inside of narrow cabinet

Maple table & stools

This strikingly simple playroom set is easy to build if you have the right tools and materials. Because the leg attachment needs to be very strong, you must use maple or another dense, split-resistant hardwood and make the mating surfaces absolutely flat.

We show laminated maple countertop for the table and edge-joined maple boards for the stools, but the materials can be used interchangeably. You can also vary the sizes of both the tops and the legs. In fact, it's best to customize their dimensions to suit both the child and the materials available. You'll need a plug cutter to cut the plugs.

1. Cut table and stool tops **A**, **C**, and **E** to size, or make the tops by edge-joining individual boards (see page 45). Round the corners as shown. Cut legs **B**, **D**, and **F** to length, making sure all cuts are square and mating surfaces are absolutely flat. Round over all long edges as shown (a router with a ½-inch or ¾-inch rounding-over bit is ideal for this).

2. Mark leg locations on the underside of each top, and mark screw locations on the upper surface (see Detail 1). For each table leg only, add a third screw, dead center. With the legs held in position, drill counterbore and pilot holes as shown in Detail 2. Glue the mating surfaces and screws, then drive in the screws (a hand brace or an electric drill with a screwdriver bit is extremely helpful here). Cut ½-inch-diameter walnut plugs and glue them over the screws.

3. When the glue has cured, trim the plugs a little "proud" of the surface, then sand them flush. Finally, sand all surfaces and finish. (Note: Maple countertop often comes pre-oiled. If you want other than an oil finish, you'll need to sand down to bare wood.)

Design: Robert Zumwalt.

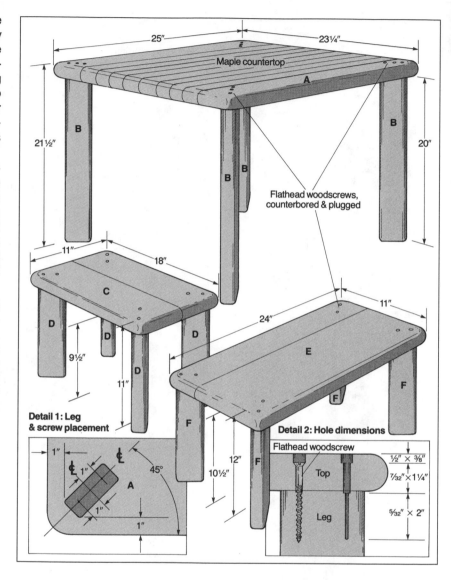

BUY		TO MAKE		
Maple (or other hardwood)				
Countertop or random-width boards (see text), 1½ inches thick	1	Table top	**A**:	23¼" by 25" (or to suit)
	1	Stool top	**C**:	11" by 18" (or to suit)
	1	Stool top	**E**:	11" by 24" (or to suit)
Random-length 2 by 4s	4	Table legs	**B**:	20" (or to suit)
	4	Stool legs	**D**:	9½" (or to suit)
	4	Stool legs	**F**:	10½" (or to suit)
MISCELLANEOUS				

¾-inch walnut (or other hardwood in a contrasting color) sufficient for 28   ½" plugs
28 flathead woodscrews, 3½" by #12 • Wood glue • Clear nontoxic finish

Elegant in its simplicity, this sturdy playset will stand up to years of use. Solid hardwood
and careful construction are the essentials for its success.

JOINERY

Joinery—the craft of assembling pieces of wood accurately and securely—is a crucial step for the success of your project.

The basic joints

The following guide explains the use and construction of the basic joints used in our projects.

Butt joints. To make these simple joints, first check that the mating surfaces are smooth and flat. Then butt one board against the other, glue and clamp, and fasten with screws, nails, or dowels (see facing page).

Miter joints. Two pieces cut and joined at a 45° angle make up the miter joint. Radial-arm and table saws have adjustable blades and guides that make mitering a cinch. If you're cutting miters with a handsaw, a miter box (see page 28) will aid you enormously.

Dado joints. Dadoes—rectangular grooves along a board's face—make strong, rigid joints widely used to construct drawers and join shelves to uprights.

Power tools work best for cutting dadoes. An electric router equipped with a straight bit smooths the cut as it goes (clamp a guide onto the work for the baseplate to follow).

To cut dadoes with a standard power saw blade, set the blade at the correct depth, cut the borders (using a guide), and make repeated passes through the waste wood until it virtually falls out. Finish each groove with light chisel strokes. Dado blades, available for both table and radial-arm saws, can cut a dado in one pass.

Rabbet joints. Rabbets, grooves cut along board edges, are commonly used for corners. The rabbets minimize the amount of visible end and edge grain, and because of the extra surface they offer for gluing, the joints are very strong.

It's nearly impossible to execute a long rabbet with a handsaw. Instead, use either a router fitted with a self-piloting rabbeting bit or a stationary power saw equipped with a dado or standard blade. If you're using the standard blade, cut the inside border first, then remove the waste as described above for dado joints.

To make a *stopped* rabbet, first drill the stopped end of the rabbet to the correct depth and width, then cut the rabbet. Square off the stopped rabbet's rounded end with a sharp chisel.

Doweling

Dowels don't make joints, they reinforce them. For *through* doweling, such as for the rocking lion on pages 6–7 and the table and desk on pages 90–91 and 94–95, choose a drill bit the same diameter as the dowel and bore holes slightly shallower than the dow-

Close-up of the four basic joints

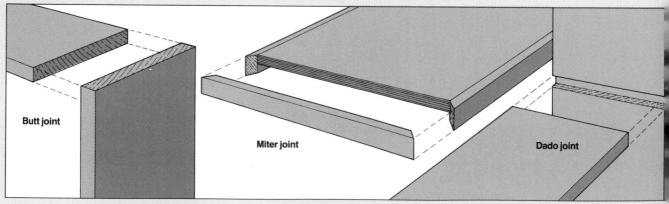

Butt, miter, dado, and rabbet are the basic joints used to assemble pieces of wood. Techniques for fastening the joints after they're cut are explained on the facing page.

el's length. Cut small lengthwise grooves in the dowel so excess glue can escape. Then coat the dowel with glue and, using a mallet or lightweight hammer, tap it into place. To finish the dowel, see at right.

Blind doweling is often used to edge-join boards when making wide panels, as required for the rocking horse on pages 8–9 and the table and stools on pages 42–43. Here, the dowels don't show; the trick is drilling straight, matching holes in the two pieces to be joined. You can do this in one of two ways. Either lay the two surfaces face to face and mark across both edges at once, then drill both holes slightly deeper than half the dowel length; or drill one hole, insert a dowel center in the hole, and press the pieces together. The dowel center marks where the second hole should be drilled. Glue the dowels as for through doweling.

A doweling jig (see page 37) makes the whole process much easier and more accurate.

Fastening techniques

Tips for fastening joints neatly and securely appear below. For information on fasteners, see page 17.

Gluing and clamping. Before applying any adhesive, always test the fit of the pieces to be glued by assembling them while dry. Make any necessary adjustments at this point.

Make sure that the pieces to be glued are clean and dry. Spread the adhesive evenly on both surfaces to be joined. The end grain of wood, which is usually more porous, may absorb extra glue; add a second coat.

Most adhesives allow for some adjustment of pieces during assembly. Check angles with a square and adjust them before the glue sets. Temporary braces made from scrap wood can be tacked on to fix angles.

When clamping, cushion the jaws of the clamp with pieces of scrap wood to avoid marring the material. Tighten the clamps until snug (but not too tight).

"Finishing" your fasteners. In most cases, fasteners need to be driven flush or concealed below the surface.

Drive finishing nails within ⅛ inch of the surface with a hammer, then tap the nail head below the surface with the point of a nailset. Conceal the resulting hole with wood putty.

Flathead and drywall screws can be countersunk or counterbored (see page 37) and covered with putty or plugs. Cut plugs from matching or contrasting wood with a plug cutter, available from many woodworking retailers.

Bolts and lag screws look best when counterbored. To drill the counterbore hole, use a bit that's the same diameter as the washer below the bolt head or nut. Drive the bolt home with a ratchet and socket.

To finish off dowel ends, trim them with a handsaw or sharp chisel, then sand them flush with the surface.

Doweling techniques

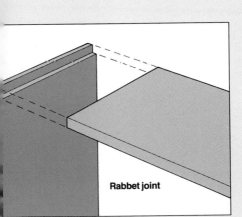

Rabbet joint

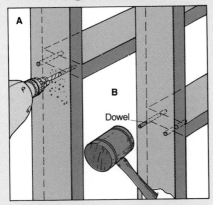

Dowel

Through doweling reinforces basic joints. First drill the holes (A), then coat the dowels with glue and tap them in (B).

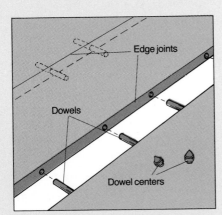

Edge joints

Dowels

Dowel centers

Blind doweling strengthens edge-joined boards. The trick is lining up the holes; dowel centers can help.

Baltic birch plywood and interlocking construction make this playset strong, lightweight, and durable; country-style pierced and painted decorations make it delightful. You can build the set from a single sheet of plywood using only basic tools and a saber saw.

Slot-together playroom set

If you prefer to spend time as a decorative painter rather than as a furniture builder, this project is for you. You can mark, cut, and assemble the entire playroom set in a day. The real fun, though, is painting the completed set.

The simple charm of folk-style furniture is evoked in each piece, and each provides plenty of "blank canvas" for decorative painting. You can use the handpainted country patterns we show or develop your own motifs. The set is ideally suited for stencil work, découpage, or the like. Each piece also knocks down easily for storage or even for shipping, which raises the interesting possibility of building the set as a gift for someone far away.

You'll need only a saber saw and basic tools; a table saw will make short work of cutting the pieces, and a router is helpful for rounding over edges, but neither is required. Refer to the drawings on pages 48–49 as you work.

Marking & cutting

1. Transfer the patterns shown in Drawing 2 to heavy paper, using the grid-enlargement technique outlined on page 36. If you wish to decorate your set as shown, transfer the leaf and apple patterns to graph paper. Cut all patterns.

2. Trace the plywood patterns onto the plywood in the areas shown in the detail drawing, then cut all pieces to size. Make angled cuts at the top of all trestles: 82° for the table trestles, 77° for the others. Cut all slots and the pierced-work apples. Round the corners of the tabletop and benchtops as shown in Drawing 1. Round over all edges, including the edges of the apple cutouts (if you have a router, use a ⅜-inch rounding-over bit set ¼ inch high). Don't round over the angled trestle tops or the slots in the trestles and chair seats.

Assembling the table & bench

1. Using stretchers **A** as patterns, mark and cut the angles at each end of bench cleat **C** and the angles at the ends of table cleats **C**. Assemble stretcher **A**, trestles **B**, and cleats **C** with screws (see Drawing 1); use ³⁄₃₂-inch pilot holes and countersink the screws. For the second table cleat **C**, drill counterbore holes where shown and ⅛-inch pilot holes for the 2½-inch screws.

2. Invert tops **D** and the **ABC** assemblies; center and mark each **ABC** assembly on its top. Remove the **ABC** assemblies and apply glue to cleats **C** only; then fasten the **ABC** assemblies to the tops with five 2d nails through each cleat, driving the nails flush (do not set the heads).

Assembling the chair

1. For each chair, make cleat **C** by ripping the 1 by 4 as shown in Drawing 1 (side view). Using stretcher **A** as a pattern, mark and cut the angles at each end of the cleat. Assemble stretcher **A**, trestles **B**, and cleat **C** as shown, drilling countersink and ³⁄₃₂-inch pilot holes for the 1¼-inch screws.

2. With a file or rasp, cut back the front underside edge of the slot in chair seat **D** until chair back **E** can be angled at 77° (see Drawing 1). With all parts inverted and correctly positioned, mark the position of the **ABC** assembly on the underside of the seat; be sure chair back **E** fits snugly against cleat **C**. Remove the back and the **ABC** assembly, and apply glue to cleat **C** only; then fasten the **ABC** assembly to seat **D** with 2d nails through the cleat, driving the nails flush (do not set the heads). Using a 1¼-inch screw, fasten back **E** to cleat **C** as shown.

Finishing the set

To finish your set as shown, you'll need 2-inch alphabet stencils and ½-inch number stencils (both available at stationery stores); enamel undercoat and flat blue enamel; red, white, green, and brown artist's acrylics or oils; and matte varnish. Be sure all paints and the varnish are nontoxic.

1. Disassemble each piece. Apply undercoat and one or two coats of blue enamel to tops **D**, seats **D**, and backs **E**. When the paint is dry, apply a coat of matte varnish to all surfaces of each piece. Allow the varnish to dry thoroughly.

BUY		TO MAKE		
Baltic birch plywood				
1	½-inch 8 by 4-foot sheet	Pieces **A**, **B**, **D**, and **E** (see plywood cutting layout)		
Pine or fir (grade to suit)				
1	8-foot 1 by 3	2	Table cleats **C**:	¾″ by 2½″ (see text for length)
		1	Bench cleat **C**:	¾″ by 2½″ (see text for length)
1	2-foot 1 by 4	2	Chair cleats **C**:	¾″ (see text for width and length)
MISCELLANEOUS				

29 drywall screws, 1¼″ by #6 • 3 drywall screws, 2½″ by #8 • 2d finishing nails
Wood glue • Finish (see text)

2. Using the photo and Drawing 2 as guides, tape the leaf and apple patterns in position, then trace lightly around each pattern with a pencil. Remove the patterns and, using the photo for reference, paint in the red, white, and green portions of the designs. Let the paint dry; then use a little brown to create shadowing on the apples, and give each one a white highlight as well.

3. When all the paint is dry, tape the alphabet and number stencils in place and paint in each character with red. Paint all exposed plywood edges red as shown. Let the paint dry.

If you have a steady hand, box in the tabletop and benchtop apples with light, ruled pencil lines, then paint over your marks with red (see the photo for guidance).

4. After all the decorative painting is completely dry, apply two coats of matte varnish to protect your work. Follow the manufacturer's instructions, but omit sanding between coats.

Design: Pamela Silin Palmer & Karen Kariya of Faunus Designs.

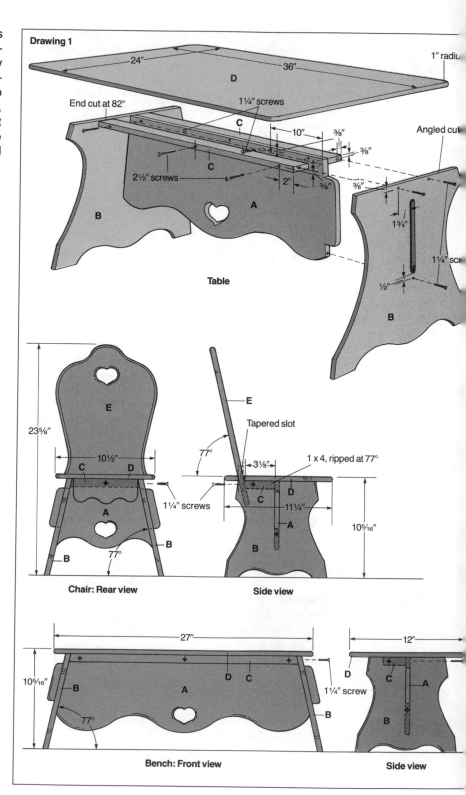

Drawing 1

Table

Chair: Rear view

Side view

Bench: Front view

Side view

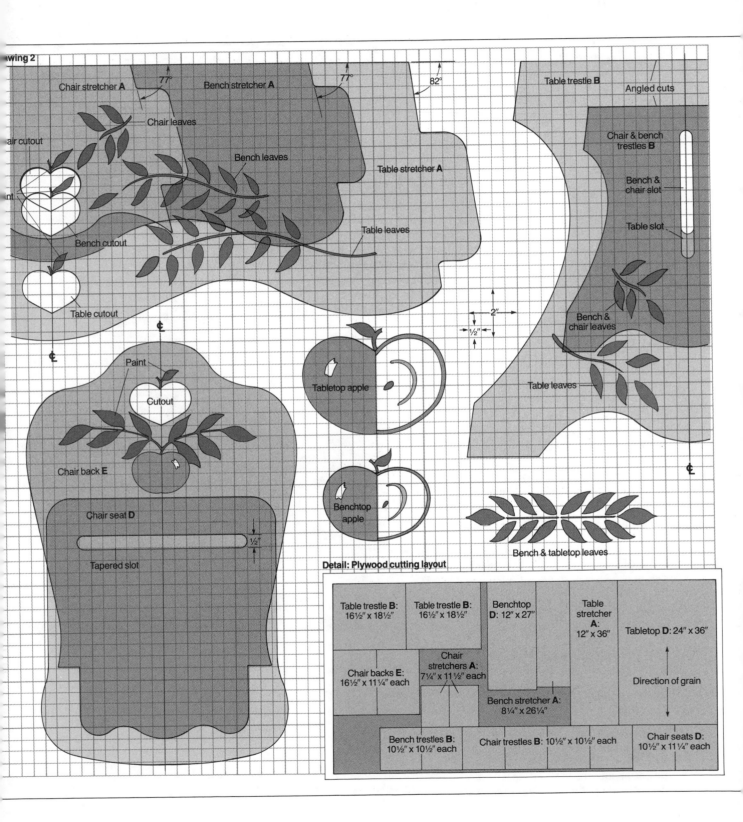

Chair stretcher **A**

77°

Bench stretcher **A**

77°

82°

Table trestle **B**

Angled cuts

Chair leaves

air cutout

nt

Bench leaves

Chair & bench trestles **B**

Table stretcher **A**

Bench & chair slot

Table leaves

Table slot

Bench cutout

Table cutout

2"

½"

Bench & chair leaves

Paint

Cutout

Tabletop apple

Table leaves

Chair back **E**

Benchtop apple

Chair seat **D**

½"

Tapered slot

Bench & tabletop leaves

Detail: Plywood cutting layout

Table trestle **B**: 16½" x 18½"	Table trestle **B**: 16½" x 18½"	Benchtop **D**: 12" x 27"	Table stretcher **A**: 12" x 36"	Tabletop **D**: 24" x 36"
Chair backs **E**: 16½" x 11¼" each	Chair stretchers **A**: 7¼" x 11½" each			Direction of grain
		Bench stretcher **A**: 8¼" x 26¼"		
Bench trestles **B**: 10½" x 10½" each	Chair trestles **B**: 10½" x 10½" each			Chair seats **D**: 10½" x 11¼" each

49

Scandinavian rocking cradle

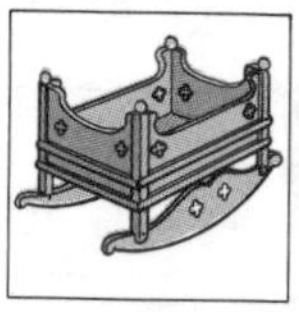

This pretty cradle takes its design from traditional Norwegian folk cradles. It features graceful curves, pierced decoration, and a soothing end-to-end rocking motion that mimics the rise and fall of a boat on a gentle swell.

We've specified clear pine and a clear finish, but there are many other possibilities you might consider. Old Norwegian cradles were often painted or were finished with both paint and a natural finish. Sometimes, a decorative band of carved or painted patterns was added at the base of the cradle.

Our design allows for all these possibilities. For example, you might want to paint or stain your cradle—translucent colors that let the grain show through are especially attractive. If you're fond of stenciling, carving, or decorative painting, consider attaching the band at the bottom of the cradle.

Even though we've specified clear pine for best appearance, almost any kiln-dried grade will do; just select the pieces carefully.

The cradle is sized to take a standard 18 by 36-inch cradle mattress. Construction is simple and requires only basic tools. A radial-arm or table saw, or a router, is helpful for cutting the rabbets; the router also makes it easier to round over edges. Use a hole saw or Forstner bit for the pierced quatrefoil decorations.

The only tricky cut in the project is the stopped rabbet in each post; see page 44 for instructions. Take special care in cutting and rabbeting all the cradle pieces. Opposite sides must match exactly, and the rocker bottoms must have identical curves for a smooth rocking action.

1. Cut all pieces to size. Transfer the cutting patterns to heavy paper (see page 36) and cut them out. Then use the paper patterns to mark and cut both the left and right-side profiles in sides

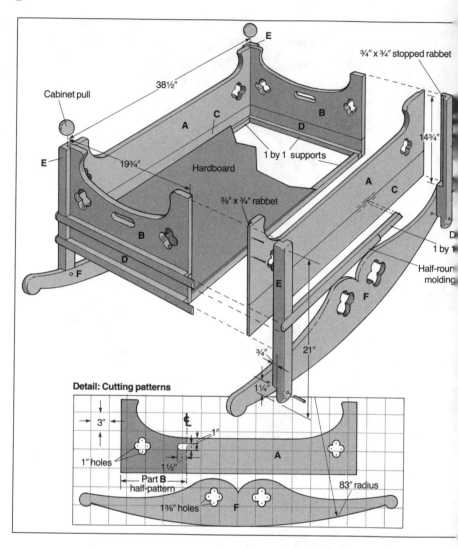

BUY		TO MAKE		
Clear pine				
2	6-foot 1 by 12s	2	Sides **A**:	¾″ by 11¼″ by 38½″
		2	Ends **B**:	¾″ by 11¼″ by 19¾″
2	6-foot 1 by 4s	2	Sides **C**:	¾″ by 3½″ by 38½″
		2	Ends **D**:	¾″ by 3½″ by 19¾″
1	8-foot 2 by 2	4	Posts **E**:	1½″ by 1½″ by 21″
1	10-foot 1 by 8	2	Rockers **F**:	¾″ by 7¼″ by 51″
6	6-foot 1 by 1s	Trim and hardboard supports (see text)		

MISCELLANEOUS

4 pieces of ¾″ half-round pine molding, each 6′ long • 9″ of ½″ hardwood dowel
4 cabinet pulls, 1½″ in diameter • 1 piece of ¼″ hardboard, 18¾″ by 36¾″
3d finishing nails • Wood glue • Clear nontoxic finish • Cradle mattress, 18″ by 36″

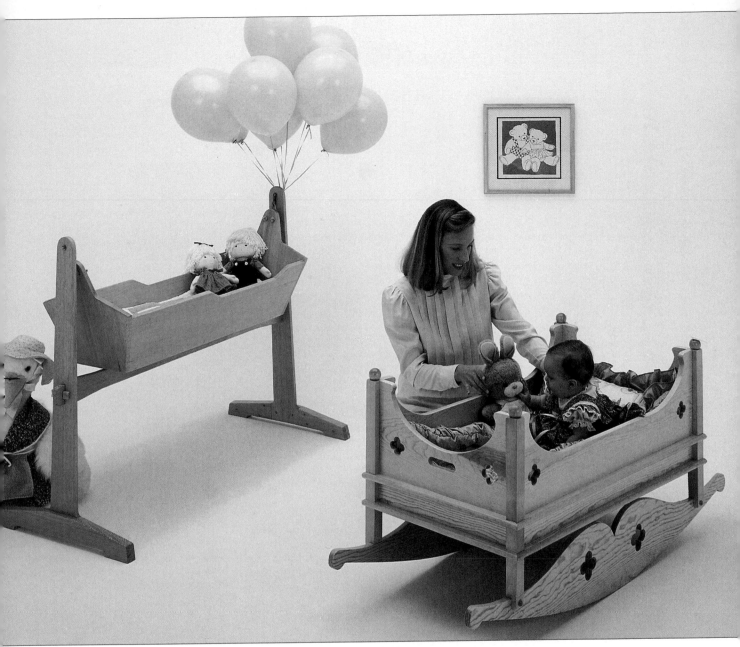

These two cradles are based on timeless designs from two different cultures: at left, a graceful, Shaker-style hanging cradle made from clear fir; at right, a cozy, Scandinavian rocking cradle made from clear pine. Each is direct and simple in both concept and construction.

…Scandinavian rocking cradle

A, ends **B**, and rockers **F** (flip the paper patterns over to get the right-side profiles of ends **B**). Mark and cut quatrefoils in **A**, **B**, and **F**. Rabbet sides **A** and **C** and posts **E**. Round the bottoms of the posts as shown and cut hand-holds in ends **B**.

2. Glue and nail together sides **A** and ends **B**; repeat for **C** and **D**. Square-up the resulting frames and let the glue cure. Glue posts **E** to the **CD** box, then add the **AB** box, gluing it to posts **E** and the **CD** box. Let the glue cure.

3. Measure and cut the 1 by 1s and half-round trim to fit as shown, allowing the longer half-rounds to extend ½ inch beyond the edge. (Note: You may need to rip the 1 by 1s to get an exact fit between the cradle sides and the half-rounds.) Glue all the trim in place. When the glue has cured, trim and round over the protruding half-rounds. Use the remaining 1 by 1s to provide hardboard supports as shown. Glue and nail the supports flush with the bottom of the sides and ends.

4. Clamp rockers **F** in place, then mark and drill **E** and **F** where shown for dowel connectors. Cut four 2-inch dowel pieces and round over one end of each. Glue and dowel the rockers to the posts. Glue a cabinet pull to the top of each post. Sand, then apply the finish of your choice. When the finish is dry, drop in the hardboard mattress support and add the mattress.

Design: Scott Fitzgerrell.

Shaker-style hanging cradle

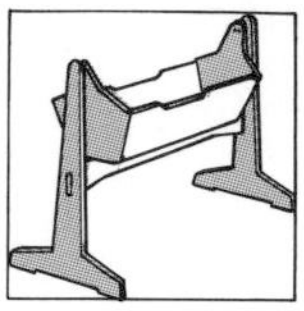

This traditional cradle adapts the simple lines of old Shaker cradles, lines that make it at once easy to build and easy to look at. Like many antique cradles, it uses a long, narrow mattress that helps restrain very young infants and provides room at the foot for toys and extra bedding. The cradle, pictured on page 51, unclips from its stand; the stand knocks down for travel or storage.

To make the cradle, you'll need basic tools and a saber or circular saw—or preferably a radial-arm or table saw. Construction, though requiring precision, is essentially easy.

1. Rip one eased edge from the 6-foot 1 by 10. Cut all pieces to size; cut the dowel into six 2-inch and two 2¼-inch pieces. Edge-join ends **A** to make two 17 by 18¼-inch panels, blind doweling with the 2-inch dowels (see Detail 3 and page 45).

Referring to the large drawing and Details 2 and 3, make bevel and profile cuts in ends **AA** and sides **B**, bottom **C**, and stretcher **G**. Drill two ¼-inch holes in each end **AA** where shown. Add dowels in the ends of stretcher **G** (see Detail 2). With ½-inch and ¾-inch drill bits and a chisel, file, or rasp, make rectangular mortises in uprights **D** and stretcher **G** where shown. From scrap wood, make four wedges as shown in Detail 2.

2. Spacing nails every 2 to 3 inches, glue and nail ends **AA** to sides **B**, then fasten bottom **C** in place. Glue and screw uprights **D** to crosspieces **E**, then glue and nail crosspieces **F** in place as shown. When the glue has cured, mark and cut the foot and upright profiles as shown in the large drawing and Detail 1. Drill ¼-inch holes in the uprights where shown.

3. Round over all edges (except the wedges), then set the nails and fill the holes. Sand smooth. Apply the finish of your choice (we used polyurethane). When the finish is dry, bolt the snap hooks in place; cut the bolt ends flush with the nuts and peen smooth.

4. To assemble, insert stretcher **G** in uprights **D** and gently tap in the wedges. For extra security, add screws (see Detail 2), countersinking the heads. Add loops of rope to the cradle, adjusting the length so the cradle bottom clears the stretcher; secure each end with overhand knots. (Heat the rope ends with a match to prevent fraying.) Clip the cradle in place and add the mattress.

Design: Randall Fleming & Scott Fitzgerrell.

BUY		TO MAKE			
Clear fir or pine					
1	6-foot 1 by 10	4	Ends	**A**:	¾″ by 9⅛″ by 17″
1	10-foot 1 by 10	2	Sides	**B**:	¾″ by 9¼″ by 39″
		1	Bottom	**C**:	¾″ by 9¼″ by 36″
2	8-foot 1 by 6s	2	Uprights	**D**:	¾″ by 5½″ by 40″
		2	Crosspieces	**E**:	¾″ by 5½″ by 24″
		4	Crosspieces	**F**:	¾″ by 5½″ by 9¼″
1	6-foot 1 by 4	1	Stretcher	**G**:	¾″ by 3½″ by 50½″

MISCELLANEOUS
2 bronze snap hooks, 2¼″ long • 2′ of ¼″ hardwood dowel
3′ of ¼″ bronze-colored nylon rope (check marine supply stores)
2 roundhead brass bolts, ¼″ by 1½″, with nuts and washers
10 drywall screws, 1¼″ by #6 • 3d finishing nails • Wood putty • Wood glue
Clear nontoxic finish • Foam mattress, 2″ by 8½″ by 33″

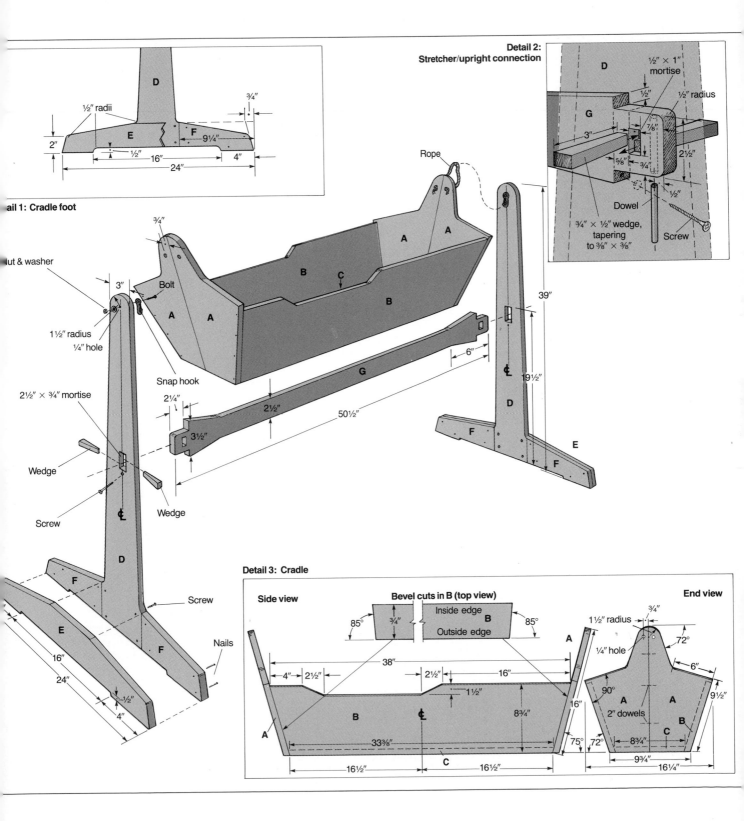

This easy-to-build system allows for plenty of imaginative play for active minds and bodies, and its three components can be arranged to fit in almost any room. The bed accepts a standard crib mattress, which is large enough for children up to early school age; a second crib mattress hides under the loft platform, ready to be set out for an overnight guest. The ramp and loft take on different identities with every new game.

Sleep & play structure

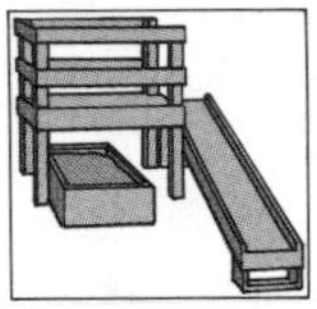

Transform an ordinary room into a fort, a castle, or any other magical place your child's imagination might create. This play/sleep structure, consisting of a loft, a bed, and a ramp/slide for traveling between the two, sets the stage for creative play and sweet dreams.

Because the bed uses a crib mattress, it's suitable only for children up to early elementary school age. When your child outgrows the bed, you can replace it with a larger one.

The bed can fit completely under the loft or be pulled out into the room as shown. A second mattress, stored under the loft platform, nestles into the loft for friends sleeping over.

In addition to basic tools, you'll need a radial-arm or table saw and a router for rounding over sharp edges. A dado blade would be helpful.

Refer to the drawings on pages 56–57 as you work.

The ramp

1. Cut ramp pieces **A–H** to size. Dado a ⅜-inch-deep by ½-inch-wide groove along the length of side rails **D** where shown. Make the angled cuts on legs **A** and **B** and side rails **D** (see detail drawing). With a ⅜-inch-radius bit, round over the upper edges of **D**.

2. Apply glue along the dadoes and insert ramp base **E**. Glue supports **F** to base **E**; then screw through the side rails **D** into the ends of **F**. Glue and nail one ramp foot **C** to ramp legs **A**, then attach the other **C** to ramp legs **B**, using 6d nails. Glue and screw ramp supports **G** to ramp legs **A** and **B**. Countersink the screws.

3. Glue and nail the feet assemblies to **D**, setting the nails. Cut one long edge of ramp end **H** at a 75° angle, then glue and nail it in place as shown.

4. Fill the nail holes, sand, and finish.

The bed

1. Cut bed pieces **I–M** to size. Glue and nail supports **K** and **L** to sides **I** and **J** as shown.

2. Glue and nail **I** to **J** at the corners, using 6d nails spaced 3 inches apart. Set the nails and fill the holes.

3. Drop bed base **M** in place.

4. Sand and finish to match the ramp; add a crib mattress.

The loft

1. Cut loft pieces **N–T** to size. Mark legs **N** for placement of all connecting rails. Drill countersink and pilot holes in rails **O** and **R** where shown. Glue and screw rails **O** and **R** in place. Countersink the screws. Glue and screw rail **S** at the bottom of one long side. Countersink the screws.

2. Drill screw holes for rails **P** and **Q** (do not attach). Notch loft base **T** as shown to fit around the legs.

3. Sand and finish to match the ramp and bed.

4. Move all the pieces into the room; then screw rails **P** and **Q** to the legs. Countersink the screws. Attach a pair of screw-eyes to the inside of each rail **O** as shown. Stretch shock cords across to hold the extra mattress. Add base **T**.

Design: Don Vandervort.

BUY		TO MAKE		
Clear pine or Douglas fir				
1	10-foot 1 by 2	2	Bed supports **L**:	¾" by 1½" by 51"
1	6-foot 1 by 2	2	Bed supports **K**:	¾" by 1½" by 28½"
1	6-foot 1 by 3	1	Loft rail **S**:	¾" by 2½" by 54½"
1	2-foot 1 by 4	1	Ramp end **H**:	¾" by 3½" by 22½"
3	10-foot 1 by 6s	4	Loft rails **R**:	¾" by 5½" by 54½"
		2	Loft rails **Q**:	¾" by 5½" by 34½"
		2	Ramp feet **C**:	¾" by 5½" by 21"
2	10-foot 1 by 6s	2	Ramp rails **D**:	¾" by 5½" by 97½"
1	10-foot 1 by 8	2	Loft rails **O**:	¾" by 7¼" by 54½"
1	6-foot 1 by 8	2	Loft rails **P**:	¾" by 7¼" by 34½"
2	8-foot 1 by 12s	2	Bed sides **J**:	¾" by 11¼" by 54"
		2	Bed sides **I**:	¾" by 11¼" by 28½"
1	10-foot 2 by 2	3	Ramp supports **F**:	1½" by 1½" by 21"
		2	Ramp supports **G**:	1½" by 1½" by 18"
4	6-foot 2 by 3s	4	Loft legs **N**:	1½" by 2½" by 70¼"
1	8-foot 2 by 6	2	Ramp legs **A**:	1½" by 5½" by 32¼"
		2	Ramp legs **B**:	1½" by 5½" by 9¾"
Fir plywood (grade AD)				
3	½-inch 4 by 8-foot sheets	1	Ramp base **E**:	½" by 21¾" by 96"
		1	Bed base **M**:	½" by 28½" by 52½"
		1	Loft base **T**:	½" by 34½" by 56"

MISCELLANEOUS
4d finishing nails • 6d finishing nails • 50 drywall screws, 2" by #6
4 2" screw-eyes • Wood glue • 2 elastic shock cords
Wood putty • Clear penetrating oil finish • 2 crib mattresses, each 27¼" by 52"

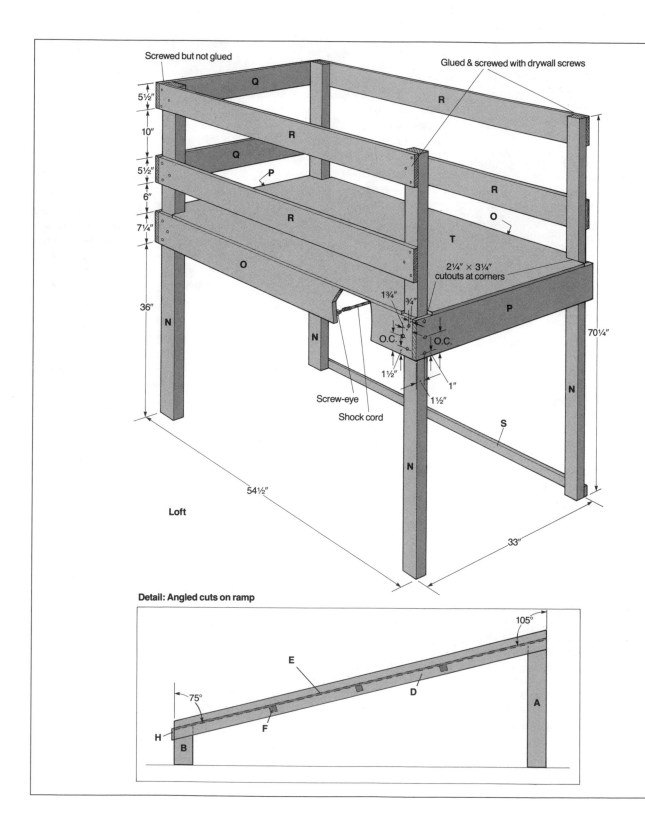

Screwed but not glued

Glued & screwed with drywall screws

Q

R

5½"

10"

R

Q

5½"

P

6"

R

7¼"

O

T

O

2¼" × 3¼"
cutouts at corners

36"

1¾"

¾"

N

N

70¼"

O.C.

O.C.

P

1½"

1"

Screw-eye

N

1½"

Shock cord

N

S

54½"

Loft

33"

Detail: Angled cuts on ramp

105°

E

D

75°

A

F

H

B

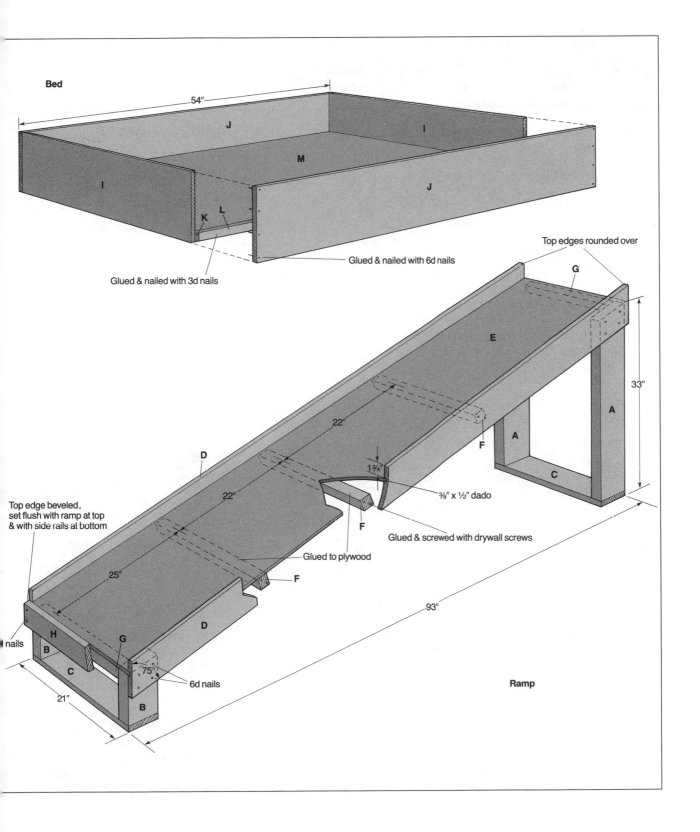

Bed

54″

J

I

M

I

J

K L

Glued & nailed with 3d nails

Glued & nailed with 6d nails

Top edges rounded over

G

E

33″

A

22″

1¾″

F

A

C

D

⅜″ x ½″ dado

22″

F

F

Glued & screwed with drywall screws

Top edge beveled, set flush with ramp at top & with side rails at bottom

25″

Glued to plywood

F

D

93″

H

nails

B

G

C

75″

B

6d nails

21″

B

Ramp

Stacking bunk beds

This bunk bed is actually two separate beds that unstack easily when the kids want a change or move into their own rooms.

The beds connect with ¾-inch dowels that are fitted into holes in the tops and bottoms of the posts. When the beds are unstacked, you can remove the safety rail and ladder and fit caps onto the tops of the posts.

For this project, you'll need a router and a radial-arm or table saw (a dado blade is helpful). Use a plug cutter to make the plugs.

1. Cut all pieces to size except the plywood mattress supports **F**. Note that ladder legs **J** are cut at a 78° angle. Rip ⅛ inch off both long edges of end rails **C** and side rails **B**.

BUY		TO MAKE		
Clear pine or Douglas fir				
4	10-foot 1 by 2s	4	Bed cleats **D**:	¾" by 1½" by 76½"
		4	Bed cleats **E**:	¾" by 1½" by 39"
4	8-foot 1 by 6s	8	End rails **C**:	¾" by 5½" by 47½"
1	8-foot 1 by 6	5	Steps **K**:	¾" by 5½" by 16"
1	10-foot 2 by 3	2	Ladder legs **J**:	1½" by 2½" by 60"
2	14-foot 2 by 6s	4	Side rails **B**:	1½" by 5½" by 76½"
1	4-foot 2 by 6	1	Safety rail **G**:	1½" by 5½" by 44"
4	8-foot 4 by 4s	8	Posts **A**:	3½" by 3½" by 40"
		8	Post caps **L**:	3½" by 3½" by 4½"
Fir plywood (grade AD)				
2	¾-inch 4 by 8-foot sheets	2	Mattress supports **F**:	Cut to fit
Hardwood dowel				
2	¾-inch by 36-inch lengths	2	Safety rail connectors **H**:	11"
		8	Post connectors **I**:	5"

MISCELLANEOUS
52 drywall screws, 2" by #6 • 24 lag screws, ¼" by 3", with washers
3d finishing nails • Wood glue • Wood putty • Clear penetrating oil finish
2 twin mattresses, each 39" by 75"

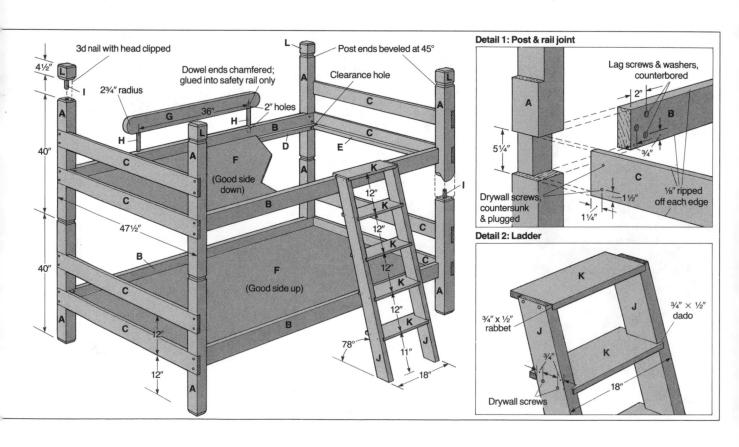

3d nail with head clipped

4½"

2¾" radius

Dowel ends chamfered; glued into safety rail only

36"

2" holes

Post ends beveled at 45°

Clearance hole

40"

47½"

40"

(Good side down)

(Good side up)

12"

12"

12"

12"

12"

12"

78°

11"

18"

Detail 1: Post & rail joint

Lag screws & washers, counterbored

2"

5¼"

¾"

Drywall screws, countersunk & plugged

1½"

1¼"

⅛" ripped off each edge

Detail 2: Ladder

¾" × ½" rabbet

¾" × ½" dado

¾"

Drywall screws

18"

The classic over-and-under combination gets two different treatments here. At left, the handsome solid-wood bunks come apart to make a pair of twin beds; at right, the lower bunk is set at a right angle to the upper one, creating space for an adjustable corner desk.

. . . Stacking bunk beds

2. Dado posts **A** to receive rails **B** and **C**—two posts as shown in Detail 1 and two posts in the mirror image for each bed. Center and bore 3-inch-deep, ¾-inch-diameter holes into both ends of all the posts. Slightly bevel all post ends with a router and chamfer bit.

3. Drill counterbore and pilot holes for lag screws in side rails **B** and countersink holes for drywall screws in end rails **C**. Glue and screw rails **C** to posts **A**; cover the screws with plugs cut from pieces of scrap lumber. Temporarily lag screw side rails **B** in place. Drill ¾-inch clearance holes for lag screws in cleats **D** as shown. Then glue and nail cleats **D** and **E** to rails **B** and **C**. Cut mattress supports **F** to fit.

4. Dado and rabbet ladder legs **J** for steps **K** at a 78° angle as shown in the large drawing and Detail 2. Glue and screw the steps in place.

5. Round the ends of safety rail **G** at a 2¾-inch radius, drill holes, and glue in safety rail connectors **H** where shown. Center and drill matching holes in one long side rail **B** to receive the dowels.

6. Insert four post cap connectors **I** into four post caps **L**. Add a nail next to the dowel in each and clip off the head (this keeps the cap from turning).

7. Sand and finish.

8. Move the bed to the room after removing the mattress supports and long rails. Reattach the rails to the end assemblies and add the mattress supports. Insert the remaining post connectors **I** into the tops of the posts of the lower bunk bed. Stack the beds. Add the post caps and the twin-size mattresses.

Design: Don Vandervort.

L-shaped bunks with adjustable desk

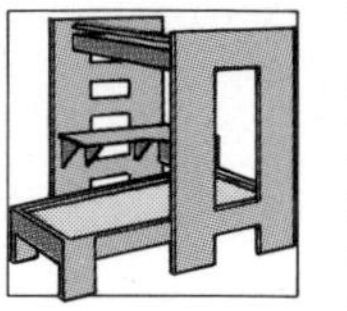

The L-shaped configuration of these bunk beds makes maximum use of minimum floor space. Not only is there the usual pair of beds, but there's also a corner desk that adjusts in height.

Construction is easy. A socket wrench, a saber or circular saw, and basic tools are all you need.

1. Cut all pieces to size. Mark and drill the counterbore and bolt holes as shown in Detail 1. Make cutouts, holes, and slots in uprights **F** and **G** and braces **K** and **M** where shown. Cut the fir round 81½ inches long; cut the dowel in half. Divide the corner guard molding into four equal lengths.

2. Except where noted, all screw connections are counterbored and filled. Glue and screw the upper and lower bed frames together as shown. Cut 1 by 2 cleats to fit each frame as shown; glue and nail them in place. Nail mattress supports **O** in position. Glue and screw legs **E** to the lower bunk.

3. Using glue and nails spaced 3 to 4 inches apart, build **HIJ** (position **J** 2¼

inches back from the rear edges of **H** and **I**), **KLMN**, and **NMN** assemblies (see Detail 3). Glue and toenail all assemblies together as shown; set the nails. Cut the screen molding as indicated and fasten with glue and brads.

4. Fill the screw holes and finish as desired. (We used satin polyurethane and semigloss enamel.) Fasten the corner guard with glue and brads.

5. Move the components into the room. With the unit on its back, position the upper bed frame and uprights **F** and **G**. Drill through the bolt holes and plywood with a ⅛-inch bit, then back through the plywood with a ¼-inch bit. Bolt the frame in place. Screw side **A3** in position where shown. Stand the unit up and attach the lower bed frame just as you did the upper one. Position the unit, locate the studs, and fasten side **A2** to the studs with lag screws. Add the fir round and secure it with dowel pins in ½-inch holes.

Drill holes for the desk-mounting bolts in upright **F** and side **D1** as you did the bunks. Bolt the desk in position. Add the mattresses.

Design: Scott Fitzgerrell.

BUY		TO MAKE			
Douglas fir (Select Structural grade)					
7	8-foot 2 by 8s	3	Sides	**A**:	1½" by 7¼" by 80"
		2	Ends	**B**:	1½" by 7¼" by 41"
		2	Ends	**C**:	1½" by 7¼" by 44"
		2	Sides	**D**:	1½" by 7¼" by 77"
Birch plywood (shop grade)					
2	¾-inch 4 by 8-foot sheets	Pieces **E–N** (see Detail 2)			
Douglas fir plywood (AD grade)					
2	¾-inch 4 by 8-foot sheets	2	Supports	**O**:	¾" by 40¾" by 76¾"
MISCELLANEOUS					

MISCELLANEOUS
Fir round, 1⅜" by 8' • Pine or fir corner guard molding, ¾" by ¾" by 6'
2 pieces of ¼" by ¾" pine or fir screen molding, each 6' long • 4" of ½" hardwood dowel
4 pieces of pine or fir 1 by 2, each 12' long • 30 drywall screws, 3" by #8
8 drywall screws, 1¼" by #6 • 14 carriage bolts, ¼" by 2" • 3 carriage bolts, ¼" by 2½"
19 ¼" washers • 14 ¼" nuts • 3 ¼" wing nuts • 2 lag screws, ¼" by 3"
3d finishing nails • Brads • Wood glue • Wood putty • Finish
2 twin mattresses, each 39" by 75"

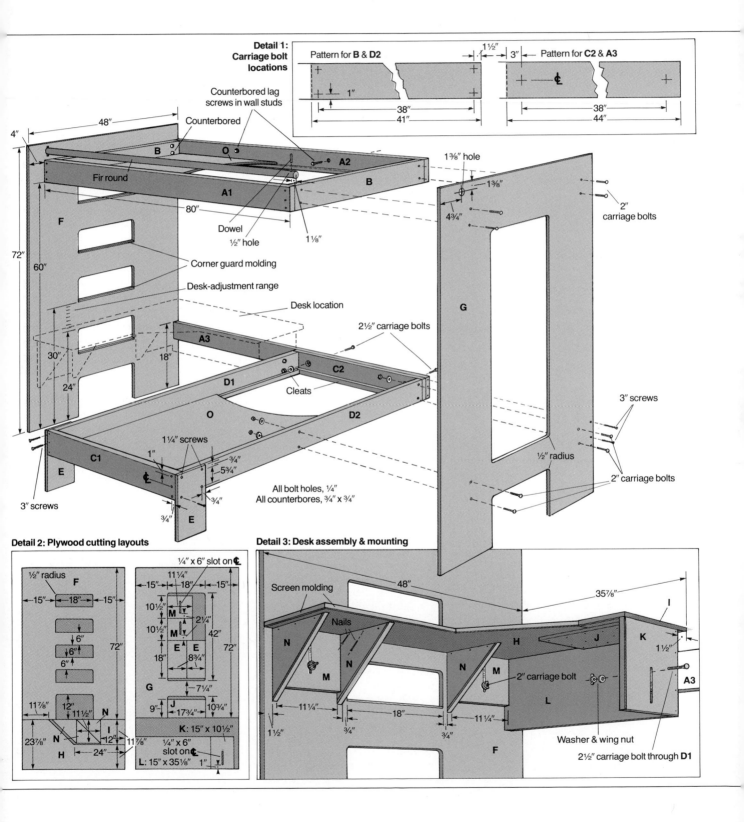

Detail 1: Carriage bolt locations

Pattern for **B** & **D2**

1½"

1"

38"
41"

3"   Pattern for **C2** & **A3**

38"
44"

48"

4"

Counterbored lag screws in wall studs

Counterbored

B   **O**   **A2**

Fir round   **B**

1⅜" hole

1⅜"

4¾"

2" carriage bolts

A1

80"

Dowel

½" hole

1⅛"

Corner guard molding

Desk-adjustment range

Desk location

F

72"

60"

G

30"

24"

18"

A3

2½" carriage bolts

Cleats

D1   **C2**

O   **D2**

½" radius

3" screws

2" carriage bolts

C1

1"

1¼" screws

¾"

5¾"

E

3" screws

¾"

¾"

E

All bolt holes, ¼"
All counterbores, ¾" x ¾"

Detail 2: Plywood cutting layouts

¼" x 6" slot on ₵

½" radius

F

15" 18" 15"

11¼"

15" 18" 15"

6"

6"

6"

72"

10½"

10½"

18"

M

M

2¼"

E **E**

8¾"

72"

42"

11⅞"

12"

11½"

N

23⅞"

N

12"

I

H

24"

11⅞"

G

7¼"

J

9"

17¾"

10¾"

K: 15" x 10½"

¼" x 6" slot on ₵

L: 15" x 35⅛"

1"

Detail 3: Desk assembly & mounting

Screen molding

48"

35⅞"

I

Nails

N

M

N

H

J

K

1½"

N

M

2" carriage bolt

A3

1½"

11¼"

¾"

18"

¾"

11¼"

L

Washer & wing nut

F

2½" carriage bolt through **D1**

Make the most of a standard metal bed frame with these two projects: underbed drawers provide useful storage in a space that's usually lost; adaptable headboards make bold graphic statements—you can use one of our motifs or design your own.

Rolling drawers

These low-profile drawers roll underneath a bed and reclaim space otherwise occupied by unmatched socks and dust balls. The drawers are perfect for storing small toys (they can be rolled to a play area) or seasonal clothing.

The feet of the bed frame must be at least 5 feet apart for all three drawers to fit underneath. If your opening is smaller, you can either change the dimensions of the fronts, backs, and bottoms of the drawers or make two wider drawers. The drawers shown use most of the depth available with a twin bed, but you can make them any depth you like. You might even make two sets, one set accessible from each side of the bed. You could also make one to fit at the end of the bed.

All three drawers are made from one sheet of ½-inch plywood. In addition to basic tools, you'll need a radial-arm or table saw. A dado blade would be helpful.

1. Cut all pieces to size (see plywood cutting layout and materials list). Cut ½-inch-wide by ¼-inch-deep dadoes along sides **A** and backs **B** where shown.

2. For each drawer, glue and nail sides **A** to back **B** and inner front **C** as shown, keeping the upper edges flush. Glue along the dadoes and slide bottom **D** into the grooves. Nail the bottom to the underside of the inner front.

3. Drill pilot holes and screw through inner front **C** into front **E**, keeping all edges flush. Countersink the screws.

4. Set all nails and fill the nail and screw holes. Sand and finish. Screw a caster to the bottom at each corner. (Note: Though the drawers can be gripped under the front, you can add a pull to each for convenience.)

Design: Don Vandervort.

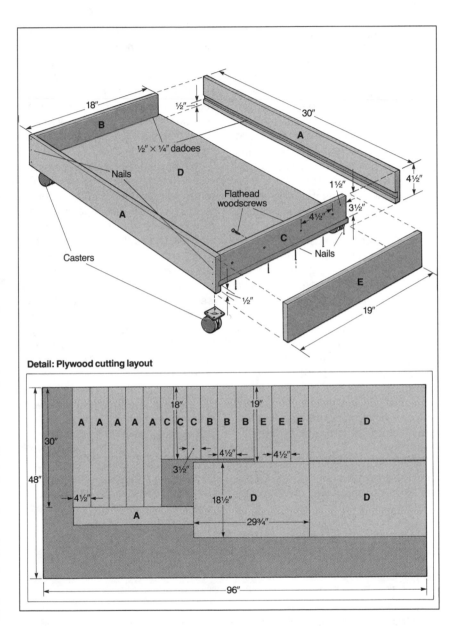

Detail: Plywood cutting layout

BUY (For three drawers)	TO MAKE
Birch plywood (shop grade)	
1 ½-inch 4 by 8-foot sheet	Pieces **A–E** (see plywood cutting layout)

MISCELLANEOUS
3d finishing nails • 12 flathead woodscrews, ¾" by #6
12   1¾" plate-mounted casters with screws • Wood glue • Wood putty
Paint • 3 drawer pulls (optional)

Easy custom headboards

Here's a quick cure for a characterless metal-framed twin bed—dress it up with a bold and beautiful custom headboard as shown in the photo on page 62. Each headboard is made from a sheet of plywood contour cut and dressed up with paint; the posts, which are optional, provide a frame for the painted design.

Only minimal carpentry skills are required. The level of painting is up to you. Of the four designs shown, both the teddy bear and landscape are fairly freeform—open to interpretation and not too time-consuming. The crayon-box design and the fanciful locomotive require numerous ruled lines and are a bit harder to execute.

You needn't limit yourself to the designs that are shown. You can just as easily reproduce a favorite illustration or photograph, or create an original design right on the plywood—even something as simple as your child's name or initials in big block letters or a graceful script can be wonderfully appealing.

You can construct the headboard with only basic tools, though you'll need a saber saw to make easy work of the contour cutting.

1. Choose your design and cut the plywood to the length indicated. (If you're working with an original design, divide its width into 12 equal segments, then use this interval to mark off vertical segments as required. Each square will equal 4 inches on the plywood. Be sure to leave sufficient clearance at the bottom for the mattress.)

Transfer the top contour, using the grid-enlargement techniques described on page 36 (you'll need only a beam compass—see page 36—for the crayon-box design). Cut the top profile; then sand and putty any edges that will show on the completed headboard.

If you're using the posts, measure and cut the 1 by 3s and the molding (see the detail drawing for construction information), but don't fasten them in place. If you're not using the posts, you can round the "shoulder" provided in each pattern and carry the nearest design line out to the edge of the plywood.

2. Undercoat all pieces and let them dry. Draw a line across the plywood sheet 18 inches up from the bottom and mark off a 4-inch grid from this point to the top of the sheet. (Note: Eighteen inches allows 6 inches each for the frame, the box spring, and the mattress; measure the bed you're using and adjust this dimension as needed

so that the painted design begins just below mattress level.) Use a pencil to transfer the gridded pattern (yours or ours) to the plywood.

3. Paint the headboard as desired. The samples shown were painted with interior semigloss enamel. Hobby-shop enamels, available in smaller quantities than house paints, are also a good choice.

We used browns, greens, yellows, pale blue, white, and red for the landscape. The locomotive was done in mossy green, crimson, black, gray, and brown; the yellow lines are vinyl pinstriping tape purchased at an automotive supply store. The tape is a real timesaver—but don't use it unless your child is past the age of peeling it off and ingesting it.

For the crayon-box design, we used a light mustard yellow, dark green, a rainbow of crayon colors, and black pinstriping tape. The teddy bear was done in tan, medium brown, white, green, and blue. Colors were mixed freely on all headboards to achieve pastels and intermediate shades; experiment with your own colors.

4. When the paint is thoroughly dry, glue and nail the post pieces in place. Drill holes for the knobs where shown in the detail drawing and glue them in place. Set the nails and fill the holes; then touch up the paint. When it's dry, you can apply one or two coats of matte or satin polyurethane or varnish to all surfaces, if you like, for maximum protection and durability.

5. Spacing the headboard ¾ inch up from the floor, use the headboard-mounting flanges on the metal bed frame as templates for marking and drilling ¼-inch mounting holes in the headboard for four carriage bolts. Bolt the headboard in place as shown. Or you can fasten the headboard directly to the wall, using hollow-wall fasteners.

Design: Sandra Popovich & Scott Fitzgerrell.

BUY		TO MAKE
Birch plywood (shop grade)		
1	¾-inch 4 by 8-foot sheet	One headboard (see text for size and shape)

MISCELLANEOUS

4 carriage bolts, ¼" by 1½", with nuts and washers • Wood putty • Finish
Twin-size metal bed frame with mattress and box spring • Hollow-wall fasteners (optional)
For optional posts: 4 pine or fir 1 by 3s, 6' long • 2 pieces of pine molding, ⅜" by 1¾" by 6'
2 wood knobs or decorative finials • Wood glue • 3d nails

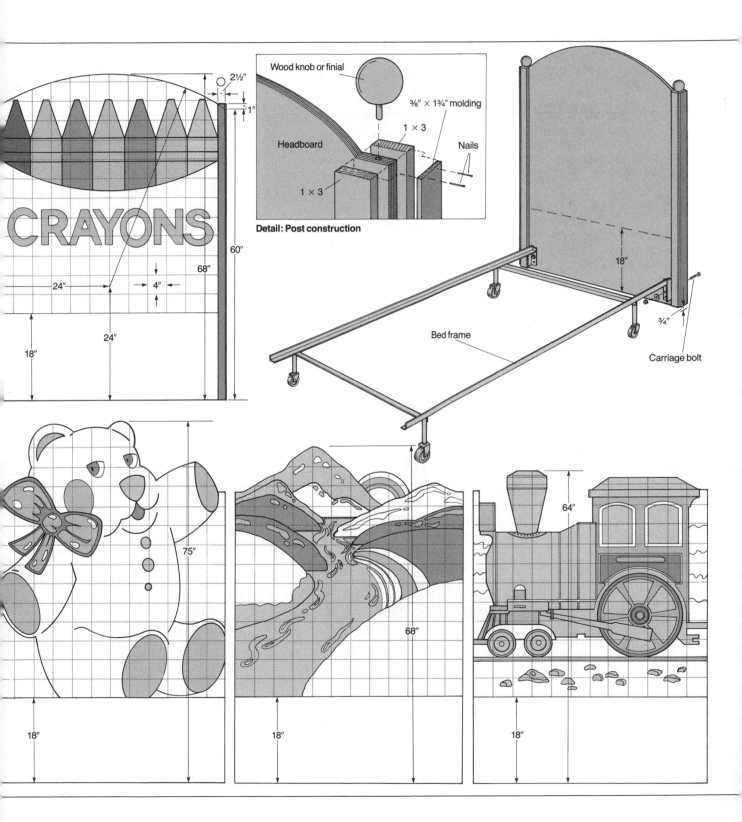

CRAYONS

2½"
1"
60"
68"
24"
4"
24"
18"

Detail: Post construction

Wood knob or finial

⅜" × 1¾" molding

1 × 3

Headboard

Nails

1 × 3

18"

¾"

Bed frame

Carriage bolt

75"

18"

68"

18"

64"

18"

Chest bed

This handsome chest bed is a real worker when it comes to storage. In addition to the generous drawers visible in the photo, there's a deep bin in the back for linens (you lift the twin-size mattress and open the lid to get to it).

The pieces are cut from good-looking Baltic birch plywood where appearance counts; where it doesn't, less expensive shop-grade stock is used. Solid cherry rails and cherry veneer behind the open drawer pulls dress up the front of the bed.

In addition to basic tools, you'll need a router and either a radial-arm or table saw. Except where noted, all joints are fastened with glue and countersunk screws spaced about 6 inches apart.

Refer to the drawings on pages 68–69 as you work.

1. Cut all pieces to size. Dado and round over top rail **N** as shown in Detail 2. Cut rabbets and dadoes in drawer pieces **G**, **H**, and **I** as shown in the large drawing and Detail 4. (Note: The length of fronts **H** and backs **I** presumes a ½-inch clearance for the drawer glides. This is standard, but check your glides to be sure.) Cut holes for pulls in drawer facings **J** and bin lid **F**. Using a router with a ½-inch rounding-over bit set ⅜ inch high, rout all plywood edges that will show. With a cove or core-box bit, rout the drawer pulls in facings **J** as

shown in Detail 3. Cut the cherry veneer into ten 3-inch squares.

2. Join long divider **A** to short dividers **B**, spacing the short dividers 25 inches from the ends of the long one. Join ends **C** to back **D**. Square-up these assemblies and let the glue cure. Then cut nine 1 by 2 cleats to fit, fastening them where indicated in the large drawing.

3. Join ends **C** to **A** as shown. Add mattress support **E**, making sure everything is square before driving the screws. Attach the continuous hinge to bin lid **F**, then fasten the lid in place. Glue top rail **N** to the mattress support; then fasten it to each end **C** with two screws on center line, spaced about ½ inch from the top and bottom of the rail (see Detail 2). Glue bottom rail **O** to ends **C** and short partitions **B**; screw through **C** into the rail, following the directions above.

4. For each drawer, attach sides **G** to back **I**, slide in drawer bottom **K** (it's not necessary to glue it), then add front **H**.

Square-up the frame and let the glue cure. Glue veneer squares on the inside of each drawer facing **J** as shown in Detail 3. Finally, glue facings **J** to fronts **H**, allowing ¾-inch overlaps at the sides, 1-inch overlaps at the top and bottom of the large drawer, and 1¹⁄₁₆-inch overlaps at the top and bottom of each small drawer. Drive six countersunk screws through each front **H** into each facing **J**, using one screw at each corner and two in the center.

5. Fill all holes, sand, and apply two coats of finish. Add bin bottoms **L** and **M** (they don't need to be fastened).

6. Attach the drawer glides, following the manufacturer's directions. The drawers overlap the ends and dividers by ¼ inch, the top rail by ⅝ inch, and the bottom rail by ½ inch. Mount the middle drawer first, then use it as a guide for aligning the small drawers. Allow a ¼-inch space between each pair of small drawers.

Design: Robert Zumwalt.

BUY		TO MAKE	
Baltic birch plywood			
1	¾-inch 8 by 4-foot sheet	Pieces **C** and **J** (see Detail 1)	
Birch plywood (shop grade)			
3	¾-inch 4 by 8-foot sheets	Pieces **A**, **B**, and **D–I** (see Detail 1)	
Tempered hardboard			
1	¼-inch 4 by 8-foot sheet	Pieces **K–M** (see Detail 1)	
Cherry			
1	2 by 4	Top rail **N**:	1½″ by 3¼″ by 76½″
1	2 by 3	Bottom rail **O**:	1½″ by 2″ by 76½″

MISCELLANEOUS
Cherry veneer sufficient for ten 3″ squares • 35′ of 1 by 2 pine or fir (for cleats)
5 pairs of 22″ full-extension drawer glides • 1 continuous hinge, 1½″ by 72″
1 lb. (about 200) drywall screws, 1¼″ by #6 • Wood glue • Wood putty
Clear nontoxic finish

When it comes to packing a great deal of storage into a small space, it's hard to beat this twin-size chest bed. Baltic birch plywood combines attractively with cherry accents, and construction is strong and straightforward.

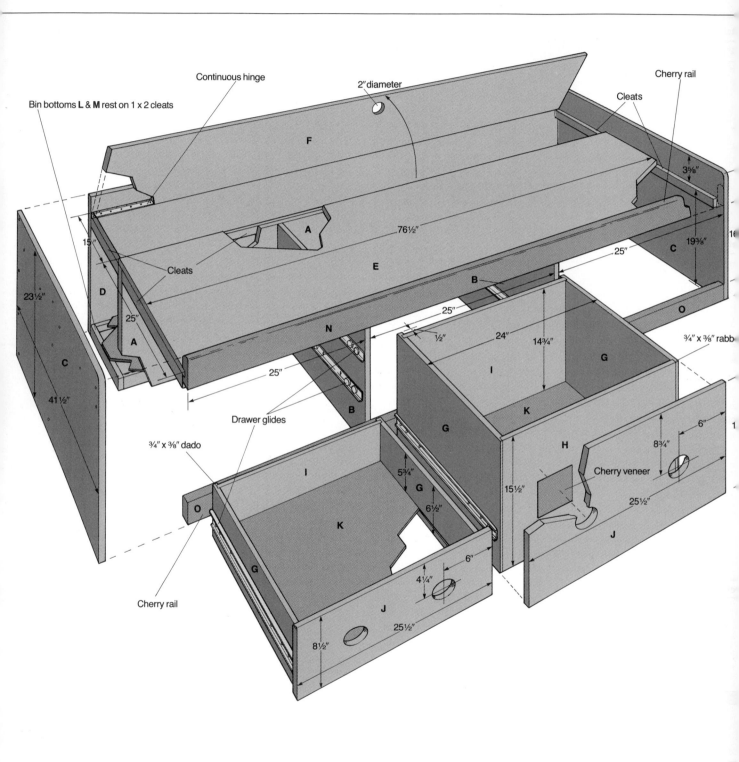

Bin bottoms **L** & **M** rest on 1 x 2 cleats

Continuous hinge

2" diameter

Cherry rail

Cleats

3⅝"

F

15"

A

Cleats

25"

19⅜"

76½"

D

C

25"

E

25"

B

B

25"

O

23½"

A

½"

24"

14¾"

¾" x ⅜" rabb

N

C

I

G

41½"

B

G

O

K

¾" x ⅜" dado

Drawer glides

I

G

5¾"

6"

8¾"

K

6½"

H

15½"

Cherry veneer

25½"

G

K

4¼"

J

6"

J

Cherry rail

J

25½"

8½"

tail 1: Cutting layouts

/4″ Baltic birch plywood

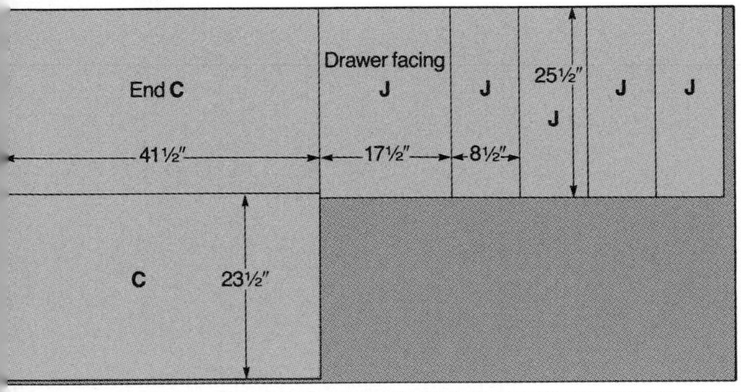

End C
Drawer facing
J
J
J
J
J
25½″
41½″
17½″
8½″
C
23½″

Birch plywood (shop grade)

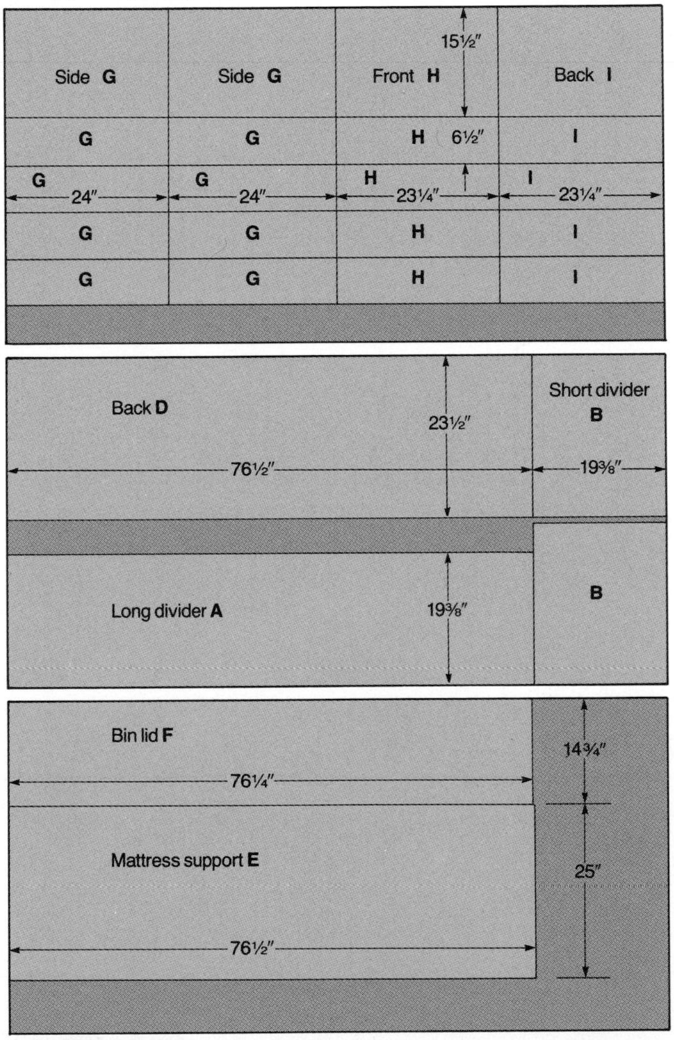

Side G
Side G
Front H
Back I
15½″
G
G
H
6½″
I
G
G
H
I
24″
24″
23¼″
23¼″
G
G
H
I
G
G
H
I
Back D
23½″
Short divider
B
76½″
19⅜″
Long divider A
19⅜″
B
Bin lid F
14¾″
76¼″
Mattress support E
25″
76½″

Tempered hardboard

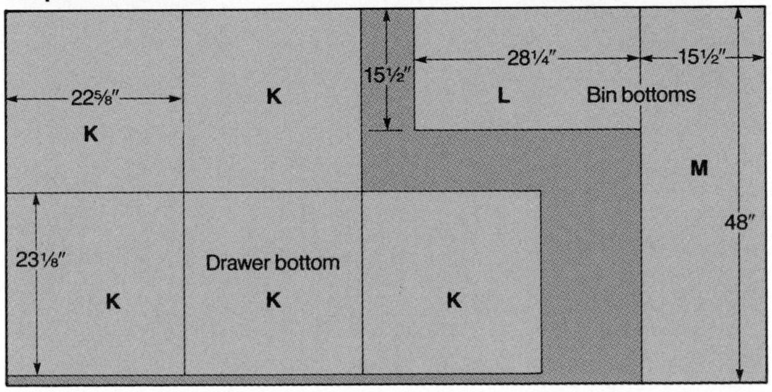

15½″
28¼″
15½″
22⅝″
K
K
L
Bin bottoms
M
23⅛″
Drawer bottom
48″
K
K
K

etail 2: Top-rail joint (side section view)

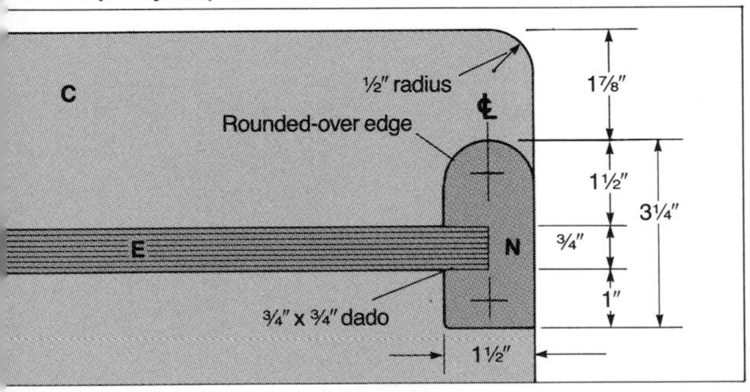

C
½″ radius
Rounded-over edge
1⅞″
1½″
3¼″
¾″
1″
E
N
¾″ x ¾″ dado
1½″

etail 3: Drawer-pull routing (front elevation & side section view)

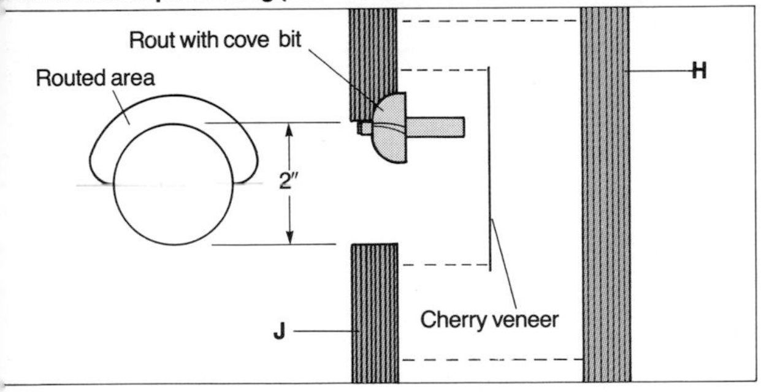

Rout with cove bit
Routed area
H
2″
J
Cherry veneer

etail 4: Drawer-bottom dadoes

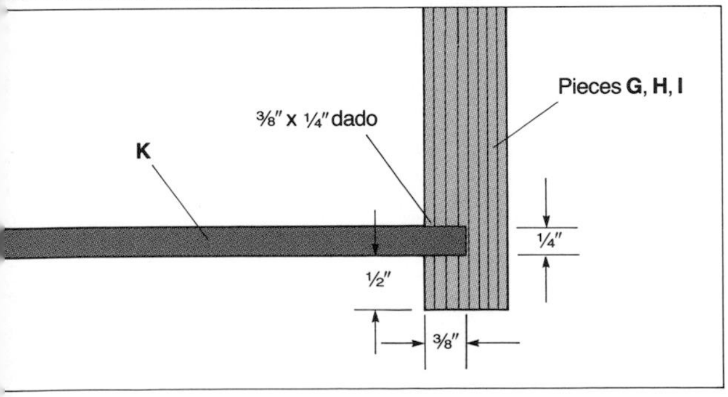

Pieces G, H, I
⅜″ x ¼″ dado
K
¼″
½″
⅜″

This enchanting canopy bed will gladden the heart of any would-be princess—and its simple, inexpensive construction will please the court carpenter as well.

Romantic canopy bed

This fanciful canopy bed, an easy weekend project that requires only basic tools to build, is essentially two frames connected by posts. One frame holds a twin-size box spring and mattress; the other supports four pairs of ready-made rod-pocket curtains (available at department stores).

1. Cut all pieces to size. Mark and drill holes in uprights **A** for finials, casters, and carriage bolts. Using the uprights as guides, drill holes for the carriage bolts in frame sides **C**.

2. Using glue and countersunk screws for all connections, attach uprights **A** to ends **B** with three screws at each joint. Then attach two cleats **D** to each side **C** (use six screws for each cleat). Assemble top frame supports **E** and **F** as shown, square the completed frame, and let the glue cure.

3. Apply the finish of your choice (we painted all plywood parts and used gold paint for the finials and clear satin polyurethane on the posts and top frame supports). When the finish is dry, attach the curtain-rod brackets (see Detail 1).

4. Move the pieces to the room and assemble sides **C** to the uprights with carriage bolts as shown. Attach the top frame to the uprights with countersunk screws (do not glue). Staple the gauze fabric to the top frame supports, letting it settle slightly between the frame members (see photo). Trim the gauze flush with the edges. Cut small holes in the gauze for the finials and insert them in the uprights. Add the box spring and mattress.

Run one curtain rod through each pair of curtains. Hang the curtains, attach the tiebacks, and add the casters.

Design: Scott Fitzgerrell.

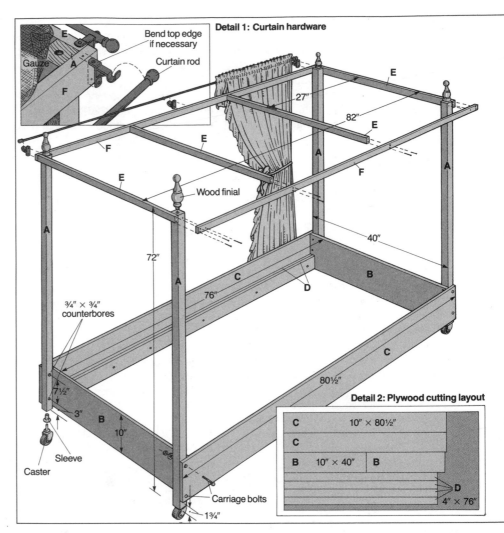

Detail 1: Curtain hardware

Bend top edge if necessary

Curtain rod

Gauze

Wood finial

¾″ × ¾″ counterbores

Sleeve

Caster

Carriage bolts

1¾″

27″

82″

40″

72″

76″

80½″

7½″

3″

10″

Detail 2: Plywood cutting layout

C	10″ × 80½″
C	
B 10″ × 40″	B
	D 4″ × 76″

BUY			TO MAKE			
Clear fir or pine						
4	6-foot 2 by 2s		4	Uprights	**A**	1½″ by 1½″ by 72″
4	8-foot 1 by 2s		4	Top frame supports	**E**	¾″ by 1½″ by 40″
			2	Top frame supports	**F**	¾″ by 1½″ by 82″
Fir plywood (grade AD)						
1	¾-inch 4 by 8-foot sheet		Pieces **B**, **C**, and **D** (see Detail 2)			

MISCELLANEOUS
4 stem-type casters, 2″ in diameter • 4 wood finials
4 pairs rod-pocket curtains with attached valances and tiebacks, 100″ wide by 72″ long
4 curtain rods • 10 curtain-rod brackets • 2½ yds. gauze fabric, at least 42″ wide
56 drywall screws, 1¼″ by #6 • 8 carriage bolts, ¼″ by 2″, with nuts and washers
Staples or tacks • Wood glue • Finish • Twin box spring and mattress, 39″ by 75″

A good finish enhances fine wood and hides the defects in lesser grades. It also keeps dirt and moisture out of wood pores and grain and wards off dents and scratches. The products used in our projects include clear finishes, enamel, and plastic laminate. Here's how to achieve good results with each one.

Preparing the wood

Before you can finish it, the wood must be carefully patched and sanded. You may also choose to seal or stain your project.

Filling and patching. Cracks, hammer marks, and fastener holes should be filled with wood putty before sanding. Spread wood putty with a putty knife or, for nail holes, your finger. Build up each patch slightly above the surface, then sand it level. When filling large or deep holes, build up the patch in layers.

Water-base wood putty, sold in powder form, allows you to "model" a surface; it's also good for filling plywood edges. Mix it with water, wet the wood surface slightly, then apply the mixture with a putty knife or your hand. The putty dries in less than an hour and sands readily.

If you plan to paint, the color of the patch isn't critical. But for a clear finish, pick a putty the same shade as the wood. If you'll be staining, choose a patch the same color as the final finish. To be sure of the best match, test the combination on a scrap of the same wood.

Sanding. The three stages in sanding are rough, preparatory, and finish. Dry, surfaced lumber doesn't require much rough sanding. Nor do the better grades of plywood—too much sanding will wear down the face veneer. A good, sharp saw blade keeps edge sanding to a minimum.

For general smoothing, choose 120-grit sandpaper; use 220-grit for finishing. For a super-smooth surface or to sand between finish coats, look for 400 or 600-grit "wet-or-dry" paper.

Sand either by hand or with a power sander. Hand sanding provides the finest finish. To provide a flat surface for the sandpaper, use a sanding block. Always sand with the wood grain; cross-grain marks will show up as ugly scratches when finished.

When the surface is smooth, dust it with a brush or vacuum, then wipe the surface with a rag moistened with mineral spirits.

Sealing. Sometimes applied to sanded wood before stain or clear finish coats, a sealer reduces moisture absorption so these later coats go on more evenly.

Shellac diluted with denatured alcohol is often used as a sealer. You'll also find a variety of special products in home improvement centers. Since sealers react differently with various stains and materials, test the combination on a wood scrap or ask your dealer.

Staining. Used for coloring wood to enhance the natural grain or make it look aged, stain also hides minor defects.

The simplest to use are pigmented oil and penetrating oil stains. Pigmented oil stains produce an opaque surface that's best for making one wood species look like another. Commonly known as colored Danish oil or colored penetrating oil, penetrating oil stains (see facing page) have become popular because they simultaneously provide color and finish coats while allowing the natural wood grain to show through.

A woodworker's finishing kit

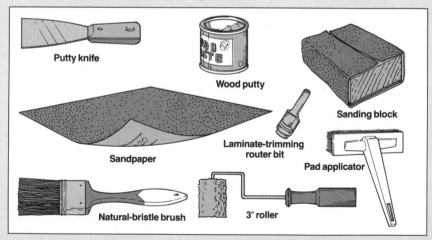

Putty knife

Wood putty

Sanding block

Sandpaper

Laminate-trimming router bit

Pad applicator

Natural-bristle brush

3″ roller

These finishing aids help you prepare, smooth, and finish wood surfaces.

Finishing techniques

Modern finishing techniques offer a wide range of appearances, from the natural look of penetrating oil to the brightest, glossiest enamel. Here's an introduction to several types. Follow the instructions on the can or ask your supplier for information on the particular product you're using.

Penetrating oil. This finish soaks into wood pores to give a natural look and feel to furniture surfaces. It's the simplest, most foolproof clear finish around.

Typically, you just spread penetrating oil on the wood with a brush or rag, wait half an hour, and wipe off the remaining surface liquid with a clean rag. A second—or even a third—application is usually a good idea, especially if the wood is very porous. The more oil absorbed by the wood, the tougher the finish coating.

If you'd like greater surface luster or extra protection, apply two or more coats of a good paste wax.

Polyurethane. A clear surface finish similar to varnish, polyurethane is extremely durable, as well as water and heat-resistant. It's available in satin and gloss finishes.

Apply polyurethane with a natural-bristle brush. To avoid a thick "plastic" look, use it sparingly, applying no more than two or three coats. Between coats, sand lightly with 600-grit wet-or-dry sandpaper or 4/0 steel wool for better adhesion. To cut excess gloss, rub the final coat with steel wool.

Lacquer. A fast-drying, high-luster finish similar to shellac, lacquer has superior durability and hardness. But its drying speed is a liability: be sure you choose a *brushing* lacquer, which dries relatively slowly.

Brush on lacquer liberally, using long strokes. Work rapidly with a wider than normal brush to speed things along. Keep your working area small and finish one area before moving on to the next.

The optimum time to wait before sanding or applying a second coat is 4 hours. After the final coat of lacquer has dried overnight, you can rub the already glossy surface with pumice or rottenstone and oil for an even higher gloss, or cut the gloss with 4/0 steel wool.

Enamel. For bright, solid colors—and for masking lower grades of wood—choose enamel, preferably oil base. It's available in flat, semigloss, and gloss finishes, and in a wide range of colors. If you need only a small quantity of enamel for a project, buy enamels in a hobby shop rather than in a paint store.

Always start your paint job with an undercoat or "primer." Not only does the undercoat seal the wood (allowing the finish coats to go on much more easily), but it also serves as an "indicator" to any remaining surface flaws, which can then be puttied or sanded. After priming, smooth the surface with 220-grit sandpaper.

Apply finish coats with a high-quality, natural-bristle brush. The trick is to spread the paint generously onto the wood, then feather it out with lighter strokes in the direction of the grain. Another technique useful for larger areas is to lay on the paint with a small (about 3-inch) paint roller, then smooth it out with light brush strokes. Pad applicators also work very well on large areas.

Let the first finish coat dry (refer to the paint can for drying time), then sand lightly with 220-grit sandpaper before applying a second, final coat.

Working with plastic laminate

If you're looking for a colorful, tough, washable surface, consider applying a layer of "childproof" 1/16-inch-thick plastic laminate. No special tools are required for the job.

First measure the surface to be laminated, adding 1/4 to 1/2 inch on all sides as a margin for error. Mark the cutting line on the laminate, then score it with a sharp utility knife. Cut with a fine-toothed saw (face up if you're using a handsaw, face down if you're using a power saw).

Apply contact cement to both surfaces to be joined and let the cement dry (normally 20 to 30 minutes). Cover the base material with heavy brown wrapping paper and lay the glued side of the laminate down on the paper. The glue, if dry enough, should not stick to the paper.

Carefully position the laminate before joining the two surfaces (once joined, the laminate can't be moved). Slowly pull the paper out, pressing the plastic down as you go. Then use a roller or rolling pin to press down the laminate.

If you're applying laminate to the edges as well as to the top surface, first attach the edge pieces, then add the top piece.

Trim the laminate to the exact size with an electric router and self-piloting laminate-trimming bit; or, if you're working with hand tools, shave it to size with a block plane, then dress it with a fine-toothed file.

73

Space shuttle bed

Like its NASA namesake, this sleek spaceship is both practical and attractive. It's at once a bed, a plaything, and a storage center. Hovering above a recessed base, the frame cradles a 33 by 66-inch standard youth mattress—a size that makes the bed compact overall, yet still suits it for children up through age 10 or 11. The base contains a drawer that can move around the room.

For all its visual impact, the bed is easy to build—it's basically just a tapered plywood box with tail fins and a curved top. Only basic tools are required, though a router, a power sander, and hand and stationary power saws are very helpful. Take time in finishing—effort expended here will pay handsomely in sculptural effect.

Refer to the drawings on pages 76–77 as you work.

1. Cut all pieces to size. Note that except for curves, you need not grid the plywood. Instead, just grid and cut one inner side **A** and use it as a pattern for cutting its mate and both outer sides **B**. Use the grids as guides for measuring the remaining pieces. The patterns do not take saw kerfs into account, since the dimensions of braces **O** aren't critical. Simply cut them from the areas shown after you've cut the other pieces. Also note that though Detail 3 gives exact measurements for the unbreak-able planters used for the rocket engines, almost any similar size will do.

2. Unless otherwise indicated, all joints are made with glue and countersunk screws set in $\frac{1}{16}$-inch pilot holes and spaced 3 to 5 inches apart. Assemble inner sides **A**, outer sides **B**, back **C**, and platform **D**. Add front bulkhead **E** after marking and cutting its angled top. Make the angled cuts on **B**.

Add side thruster mounts **F** after fitting and cutting them for best exposure of the thrusters. On each side, hold one reinforcing piece **I** in place against **A** and **F** where shown in the large drawing and Detail 3; mark and cut its junction with **B**. Set these pieces **I** on platform **D** within each thruster housing; then mark and cut each to match the curved contour of the platform. Use the completed pieces **I** as patterns for the two remaining pieces **I**.

3. Cut the 2 by 6 in thirds and glue the pieces together to form nose block **G**. Cut and shape the nose (see Detail 2); then fasten it in place.

4. Set the tips of top **H** in the tail slots. Use pieces **I** to mark and cut matching curves in the ends of **H** (**H** will overhang sides **A** and **B**; don't attempt to align it). Glue **H** into the slots, then glue and screw it to sides **A** and **B** and thruster mounts **F**, working from back to front and stopping where the downward curve begins. Space screws 4 inches apart. Glue and clamp pieces **I** in place.

Cut fifty 1-inch squares or circles from leftover $\frac{1}{4}$-inch plywood to serve as pressure pads that help bend the top. Apply glue to front bulkhead **E** and sides **A** and **B** from **E** rearward. Working from back to front, finish fastening top **H**, using screws spaced 2 to 3 inches apart and passing each screw through a pad before fastening. Let the glue cure, then remove the screws and refasten them at every other hole, omitting the pads and countersinking the screws. Repeat for the remaining length of top **H**. Trim all overhanging edges.

5. Trim the corners on main engine mounts **J** and install (see Detail 3). Glue and nail trim **K** (cut from half-round molding) in place, working from each side around to the end and cutting the pieces to fit. Butt the joints at the corners, then round them over (see the photo) with a rasp or sander. Cut louvers **L** from quarter-round molding and glue in place where shown.

6. Assemble supports **M** and **N**. Glue and nail together braces **O** and **P**, then attach to the supports as shown. Assemble drawer front and back **Q**, sides **R**, and bottom **S**. (Note: The drawer rests directly on the floor. If your floor is not carpeted, attach nonmarring furniture glides or a 2 by 4-foot piece of carpet to the underside of the drawer.)

7. Round over and putty all edges; sand well. Shape, putty, and sand the nose so **B**, **D**, **G**, and **H** all meet "seamlessly." Putty the inside angles of the thruster housings and the intersections of the tail fins and top **H**; shape the putty with your fingers or a dowel to give a coved appearance.

8. Paint carefully (see page 73). We painted our ship gloss white, the base and drawer flat black, and the engines gloss black. Decals and vinyl letters completed the job. After the paint is dry, screw the planter-engines to their mounts and add the drawer pulls.

Assemble the bed in place, attaching the supports where indicated with screws only. Drop in the mattress.

Design: Scott Fitzgerrell.

BUY	TO MAKE
Birch plywood (shop grade)	
2 $\frac{3}{4}$-inch 4 by 8-foot sheets	Pieces **A–F**, **J**, and **M–R** (see Detail 1)
1 $\frac{1}{4}$-inch 4 by 8-foot sheet	Pieces **H**, **I**, and **S** (see Detail 1)

MISCELLANEOUS

1 pine 2 by 6, 10' long • 14' of 1" half-round molding
8' of $\frac{1}{4}$" quarter-round molding • 5 unbreakable plastic planters (see Detail 3)
2 drawer pulls • 1 lb. (about 200) drywall screws, 1$\frac{1}{4}$" by #6 • 3d finishing nails
Wood glue • Water-base powdered wood putty • Nontoxic enamel • Decals and letters
1 youth mattress, 33" by 66", 4" to 6" thick

It's a straight trajectory from lumberyard to liftoff with this sleek spacecraft: you'll need little more than three sheets of plywood and basic tools. The cargo is a youth-size mattress (which keeps the overall dimensions compact). A large drawer built into the base adds valuable storage.

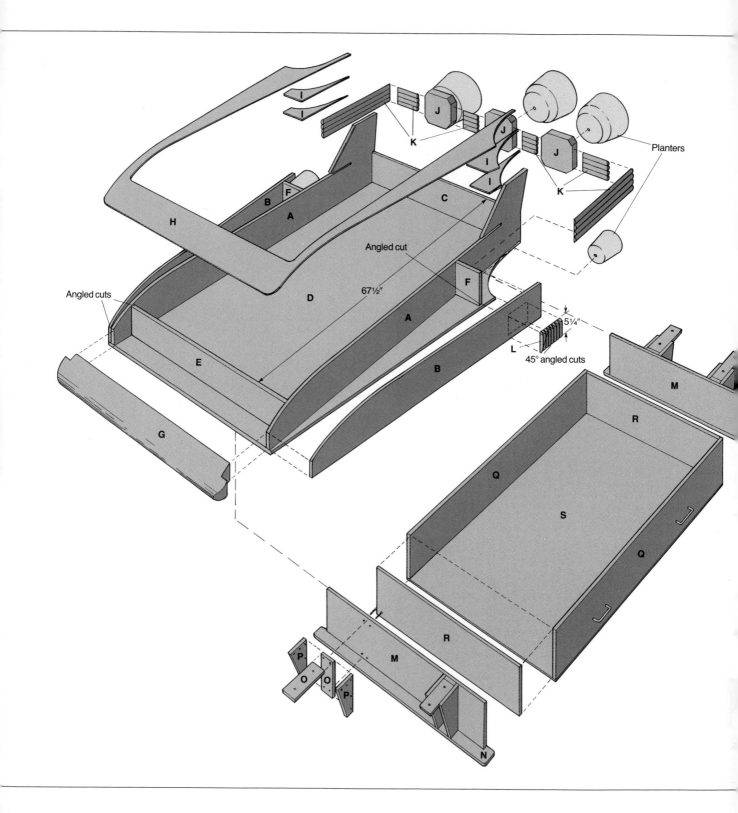

Angled cuts

I
I
K
J
J
K
J
J
I
Planters
K
B
F
A
C
H
I
F
Angled cut
D
67½″
A
5¼″
E
B
L
45° angled cuts
G
M
R
Q
S
Q
M
R
P
O
P
M
N

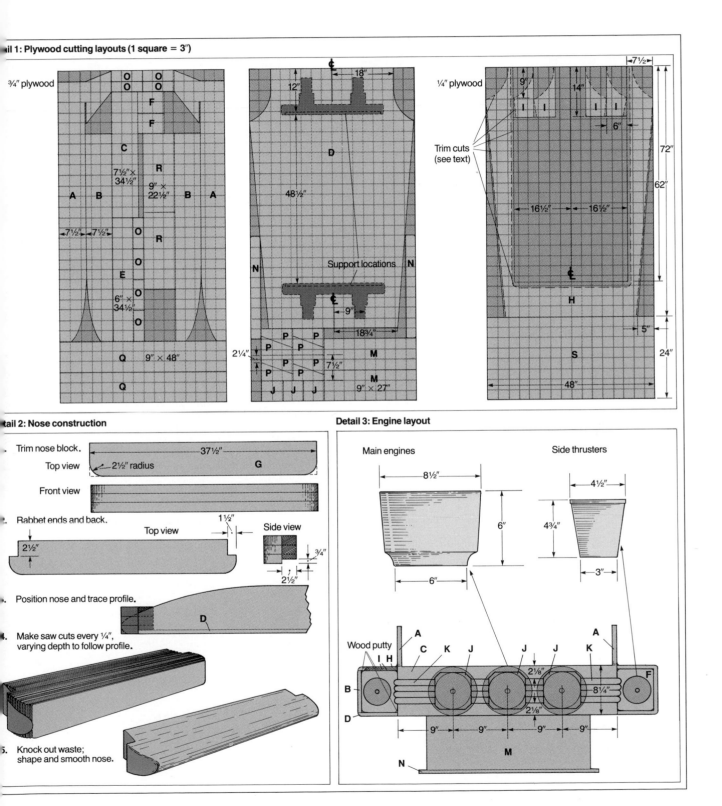

Detail 1: Plywood cutting layouts (1 square = 3″)

¾″ plywood

7½″ × 34½″

9″ × 22½″

7½″ ← 7½″

6″ × 34½″

9″ × 48″

18″

12″

48½″

Support locations

18¾″

9″

2¼″

7½″

9″ × 27″

¼″ plywood

Trim cuts (see text)

7½″

9″

14″

6″

72″

62″

24″

16½″

16½″

5″

48″

Detail 2: Nose construction

1. Trim nose block.

Top view — 37½″ — G

2½″ radius

Front view

2. Rabbet ends and back.

Top view

1½″

2½″

Side view

¾″

2½″

3. Position nose and trace profile.

D

4. Make saw cuts every ¼″, varying depth to follow profile.

5. Knock out waste; shape and smooth nose.

Detail 3: Engine layout

Main engines

8½″

6″

6″

Side thrusters

4½″

4¾″

3″

Wood putty

A

C   K   J   J   J   K   A

I H

2⅛″

F

B

8¼″

2⅛″

D

9″   9″   9″   9″

M

N

77

This tent-topped fantasy wagon has instant appeal for kids of all ages. Best suited to large spaces, it comes apart to facilitate transit between workshop and bedroom. Building the wagon is easy, but you'll need some skill to handle the tent construction.

Fantasy wagon bed

This bed conjures up a different image in the mind of each beholder. Is it a circus wagon? A camping tent? In any case, one thing is certain: the bed creates a private, almost magical place that's part bed, part clubhouse, part sanctuary.

The bed is best suited to large rooms where its bulk isn't overwhelming. It takes a twin-size mattress, but is substantially larger than a twin bed.

It's a fairly ambitious project, though only the tent construction calls for special skills. The rest of the structure is essentially a series of simple subassemblies. In addition to basic tools, you'll need a grommet tool, a sewing machine, a saber saw, and a radial-arm or table saw with dado blades. A router is also helpful.

Refer to the drawings on pages 80–81 as you work.

1. Cut all pieces to size. Using Detail 1 as a guide, drill 1¾-inch holes in frame pieces **B**. Shape the ends of handles **H** and dado the ends of legs **G**; bevel **H** and **G** where shown. Rabbet the ends of posts **L** and **M** as shown in Detail 2 (note that posts **M** should mirror each other).

For the wheels, cut the CD, CDX, and ¾-inch birch plywood into circles as shown in the large drawing (see page 37 for an easy method for cutting). From birch plywood scraps, make six 5½-inch spacers as shown, then cut a 1¾-inch hole in the center of each wheel and spacer.

2. Cut the AD plywood to 48 by 83 inches for platform **D**. Glue and nail together frame pieces **A** and **B**, using 6d nails. Square it up. Using 3d nails, glue and nail platform **D** in place, then add frame pieces **C**. Add plates **E** and **F**, fastening with glue and 6d nails. Fasten legs **G** in place where shown in Detail 1, using counterbored lag screws; do not glue. Level the platform by placing its rear edge on a sawhorse.

3. Build half-walls by gluing and nailing together **IJI** and **KJK** subassemblies as shown, using 4d nails. Glue and nail posts **M** to the **IJI** subassemblies where shown. Drilling ¼-inch holes for the bolts and ⁵⁄₁₆-inch holes for the T-nuts, fasten the half-walls to the platform with bolts and T-nuts (see half-wall framing plan in Detail 1). Glue and nail each end of the **KJK** assembly to posts **M**. Fasten posts **L** with bolts and T-nuts (see large drawing and Detail 1).

4. Measure and cut ¼-inch birch plywood for cladding to fit inside and outside the platform and half-walls as shown, butting sheets where they meet.

Fasten them with glue and brads, but don't fasten the cladding to posts **L** and don't fasten the half-wall cladding to the platform. From the 8-foot 1 by 6s, rip rail caps to fit as shown (note the mitered corners). Fasten them with 3d nails, set the nails, and fill the holes. Round over the top edges. Notch the front of the completed platform for handles **H** (see large drawing and Detail 1) and fasten the handles in place with lag screws.

5. Glue and screw together roof supports **N** and **O**. Fasten this frame to the posts with counterbored bolts and T-nuts as shown. Glue and screw together roof pieces **P** and **Q**; make an-

BUY		TO MAKE			
Fir (Clear or Select structural grade)					
2	6-foot 1 by 6s	2	Frame pieces	**A**:	¾″ by 5½″ by 48″
		2	Frame pieces	**C**:	¾″ by 5½″ by 11⅞″
4	8-foot 1 by 6s	4	Frame pieces	**B**:	¾″ by 5½″ by 81½″
1	14-foot 1 by 4	4	Wall pieces	**I**:	¾″ by 3½″ by 37″
2	8-foot 1 by 4s	2	Wall pieces	**K**:	¾″ by 3½″ by 41″
		2	Roof supports	**N**:	¾″ by 3½″ by 48½″
2	8-foot 1 by 4s	10	Wall pieces	**J**:	¾″ by 3½″ by 16½″
3	8-foot 4 by 4s	2	Legs	**G**:	3½″ by 3½″ by 20¾″
		2	Handles	**H**:	3½″ by 3½″ by 36″
		2	Posts	**L**:	3½″ by 3½″ by 38½″
		2	Posts	**M**:	3½″ by 3½″ by 38½″
5	8-foot 2 by 4s	2	Plates	**E**:	1½″ by 3½″ by 48″
		4	Plates	**F**:	1½″ by 3½″ by 35½″
		2	Roof supports	**O**:	1½″ by 3½″ by 82″
6	8-foot 1 by 2s	3	Roof pieces	**P**:	¾″ by 1½″ by 83½″
		5	Roof pieces	**Q**:	¾″ by 1½″ by 47″
2	12-foot 1 by 2s	10	Roof pieces	**R**:	¾″ by 1½″ by 28½″

MISCELLANEOUS

3 fir 1 by 6s, each 8′ long • 3 4′ by 8′ sheets of ¾″ fir plywood: grades AD, CD, and CDX
2 4′ by 8′ sheets of ¼″ birch plywood and 1 4′ by 8′ sheet of ¾″ birch plywood, all shop grade
1¾″ fir round, 5′ long • 2 pieces of ½″ hardwood dowel, each 3″ long
1⅜″ fir round: 2 pieces 44″ long, 1 piece 50″ long • 25′ of ⁵⁄₁₆″ nylon rope
75′ of ³⁄₁₆″ nylon cord • 2′ of ½″ nylon webbing • 15 yards of 10 oz. cotton canvas, 36″ wide
6 nylon fairleads and 3 horn cleats, all with mounting screws
Heavy thread • 13 ⅜″ grommets • 12 2¼″ bronze snaps (check marine supply stores)
12 hollow-wall fasteners, ¼″ drill, ⅛″–½″ grip range • 12 #10 washers
¼″ bolts: 9 at 1½″, 4 at 3½″, 4 at 4″, all with washers and T-nuts
8 lag screws, ¼″ by 3″, with washers • ¼ lb. (about 50) drywall screws, 1¼″ by #6
6d and 4d box nails • 3d finishing nails • Brads • 4 sq. inches of leather • Wood glue
Wood putty • Finish • Twin mattress, 39″ by 75″

gled cuts in roof pieces **R** and attach to **P** (see Detail 1). Glue and screw **PQ** and **PR** together and fasten the truss to **N** and **O** with screws counterbored ¾ inch. Do not glue.

6. To measure for the tent panels, use the large drawing and Detail 2 as guides, allowing at least ¾ inch at each edge for seams, 1 inch and ½ inch for hems where shown, and about 6 inches at the bottoms of the three roll-up panels. Make the hems, then sew pockets to fit the 1⅜-inch rollers. Cut six 3-inch discs from 1 by 4 scrap.

Join the panels with either simple or lapped and felled seams. Cut reinforcing triangles from the leather and attach where shown. Cut 2-inch pieces of webbing, then loop and stitch in place where shown. Install grommets in the bottom of the half-wall panels (see large drawing and Detail 2).

7. Build the wheels as shown, gluing and nailing them with 3d nails; round over the edges. Assemble the axle, spacers, and wheels; drill for and install the dowel retaining pins.

Detach the wheels and roof-truss assembly and finish all parts as desired. (We used enamel on the plywood and clear penetrating oil on the solid wood.) Glue the rope in place on the wheels, butting the ends and fastening with 3d nails if necessary.

8. Detach posts **L** and the half-wall subassembly, move all parts to the room, and reassemble. Place the tent on the frame and install the bronze snaps, fastening them as shown in Detail 2 (use the photo as a guide to spacing; fasten one snap to each post **L** with a 1¼-inch screw). Lace the tent in place with rope as shown in the photo.

Install the rollers and screw a 3-inch disc at each end. Install the cords, fairleads, and horn cleats as shown in the large drawing and Detail 2. Add the mattress.

Architect: Richard Fernau.

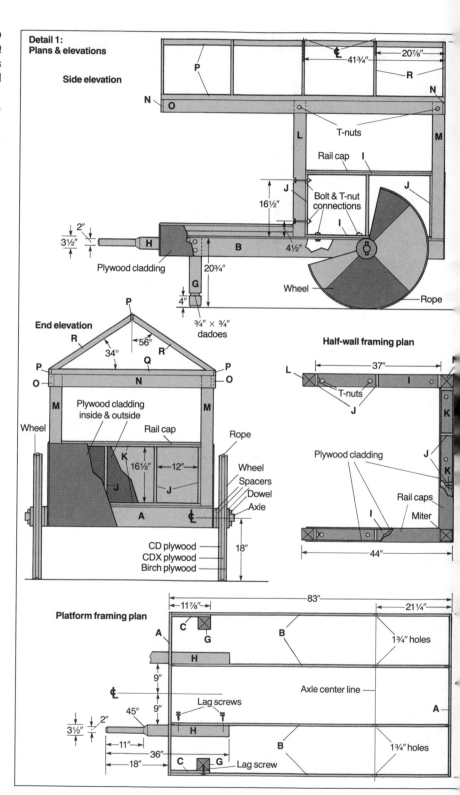

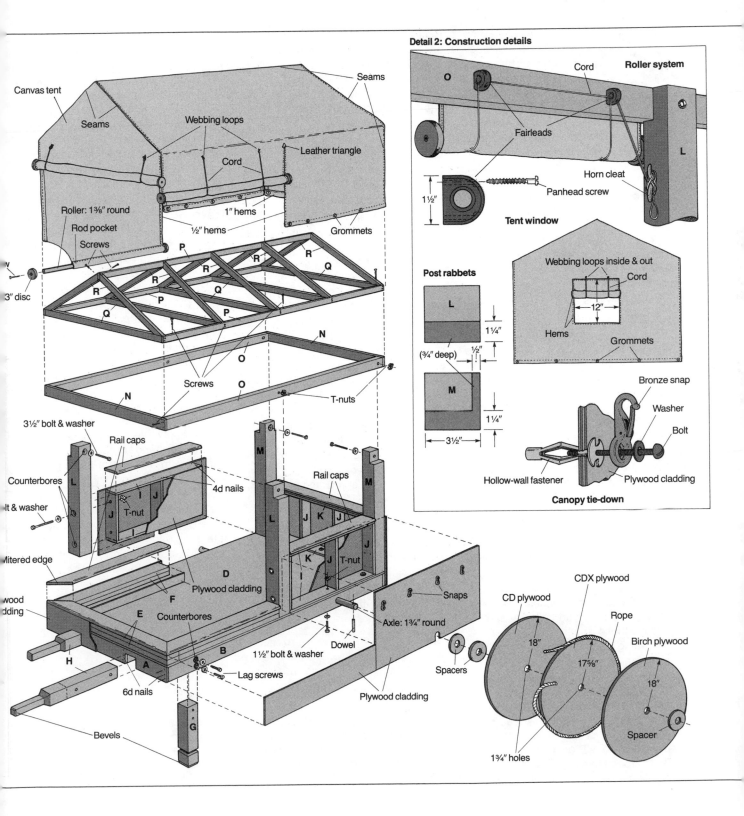

Detail 2: Construction details

Roller system

Cord

O

L

Fairleads

Horn cleat

1½"

Panhead screw

Tent window

Post rabbets

Webbing loops inside & out

Cord

L

1¼"

12"

(¾" deep)

½"

Hems

M

Grommets

1¼"

3½"

Bronze snap

Washer

Bolt

Hollow-wall fastener

Plywood cladding

Canopy tie-down

Canvas tent

Seams

Seams

Seams

Webbing loops

Leather triangle

Cord

Roller: 1⅜" round

1" hems

Rod pocket

½" hems

Grommets

Screws

P

R

R

R

Q

v

R

R

Q

3" disc

Q

P

P

Q

N

N

O

Screws

O

T-nuts

3½" bolt & washer

Rail caps

Counterbores

L

M

4d nails

lt & washer

J

I

J

Rail caps

M

J

T-nut

J

I

L

J

K

J

Mitered edge

J

K

J

T-nut

wood
dding

D

I

Plywood cladding

F

CDX plywood

Snaps

CD plywood

Rope

E

Counterbores

Axle: 1¾" round

Birch plywood

18"

H

B

Dowel

Spacers

17⅝"

A

1½" bolt & washer

18"

6d nails

Lag screws

Plywood cladding

Spacer

G

Bevels

1¾" holes

81

Race car bed

This bed is guaranteed to fire the imagination of the most avid car fan, young or old. Styled after the famous Can-Am racers, it sports such authentic details as an air dam and rear wing, fender flares, and ground-effects skirts.

The structure is similar to that of the space shuttle bed (pages 74–77); it's based on a 33 by 66-inch youth mattress, a size that suits it for children up through age 10 or 11. The bed isn't difficult to build, but it can be time-consuming. In addition to basic tools, you'll need a saber saw and a router. A radial-arm or table saw also helps.

The drawings are on pages 84–85.

1. Cut all plywood pieces to size. Note: Grid only one outer side **D** (to transfer the contours, see page 36); use this piece **D** as a pattern for cutting its mate. Make only the straight cuts in inner sides **G** and all but the angled cuts on bulkheads **E** and **F**. Cut tires **T** and **U**, and shape the wheels in outer sides **D** (see Detail 3).

Rip the 1 by 4 to 3 inches wide. Rip the 6-foot 2 by 6s to 4¾ inches wide; crosscut to make three pieces, each 48 inches long; four pieces, each 6¾ inches long; and four pieces, each 1½ inches long. Crosscut the 10-foot 2 by 6 to make two 49½-inch-long pieces.

2. Unless otherwise noted, all connections are made with glue and countersunk screws set in ¹⁄₁₆-inch pilot holes and spaced 3 to 5 inches apart. Assemble supports **A** and feet **B** as shown. Fasten these assemblies on base **C** according to the guidelines in Detail 1.

3. Position one outer side **D** and bulkheads **E** and **F**; mark **E** and **F** for the angled cuts noted in the large drawing and cut. Attach outer sides **D**, rear bulkhead **E**, and front bulkhead **F**, as shown in the large drawing and Detail 5, resting sides **D** on the projections of feet **B** (see Detail 5). Glue pieces **J** in position as shown in the large drawing.

Rest the unfinished inner sides **G** on base **C** and against outer sides **D**; trace the top contours. Referring to Details 1 and 5, mark the contours of the notched wing supports and complete the cutting of sides **G**. Fasten them in place on the guidelines (see Detail 1). Add braces **H**.

4. Build nose **O** from pieces cut from the 2 by 6s (see Detail 2). Fasten the nose in place on front bulkhead **F**. Smooth the top of the nose.

5. Attach fender flares **K** and **M**, side skirts **L** (cut from the 1 by 4), and corner pieces **N**. Rout the continuous chamfer in the flares, skirts, corner pieces, and air dam as shown in Detail 4. Hold pieces **I** in position and trace the outline of each vent opening in outer sides **D**. Cut pieces of quarter-round molding to fit within these outlines and glue them in place on **I** (see Detail 5).

6. Cut fifty 1-inch squares or circles from leftover ¼-inch plywood to serve as pressure pads that help bend the top. Glue top **P** in the slots in inner sides **G** (note that **P** will overhang sides **D** and **G**—don't attempt to align it).

Working from back to front in increments of two feet or so, glue and screw top **P** to sides **D** and **G** and braces **H**, spacing screws 2 to 3 inches apart and passing each one through a pad before fastening. Let the glue cure, then remove the screws and refasten them at every other hole, omitting the pads and countersinking the screws. Repeat for the remaining length of top **P**. Trim all overhanging edges of **P**.

7. Round over the leading and trailing edges of wing **Q** and all edges of end plates **R**; assemble **Q** and **R** as shown in Detail 5. Fasten the wing to the wing supports, then add support **S** after rounding over its exposed edges. Assemble tires **T** and **U** as shown in the large drawing and round over (see Detail 3). From the plastic pipe, cut, shape, and drill the four exhaust pipes **V** as shown in Detail 5.

8. Round over and putty all edges; fill the screw holes. Shape, putty, and sand the nose so **D**, **O**, and **P** all meet "seamlessly." Putty the inside angles of the nose, flares, skirts, wing, and wing supports; shape the putty with your fingers or a dowel to give a coved appearance (see photo).

Sand well and paint carefully (see pages 72–73). We painted our racer with a variety of enamels: high-gloss red for the body and louvers; flat black for pieces **I** and **J**, the tires, and any exposed areas of the supports and bulkhead **F**; gold metal spray paint for the wheels; and chrome spray paint for the exhaust pipes and the chair glides used as hubs and lug nuts. We trimmed our car with automotive striping tape and vinyl letters and numbers.

After the paint is dry, glue on the louver panels and tires. Install the four exhaust pipes **V** as shown in Detail 5, attaching each one with two ¾-inch screws inserted through the holes drilled in the pipe. Nail the chair glides to the wheels.

Design: Scott Fitzgerrell.

BUY		TO MAKE
Birch plywood (shop grade)		
2	¾-inch 4 by 8-foot sheets	Pieces **A–H, K, M, N**, and **Q–S** (see Detail 1)
1	¼-inch 4 by 8-foot sheet	Pieces **I, J, P, T, U**, and router base (see Detail 1)

MISCELLANEOUS

3 pine 2 by 6s, each 6′ long • 1 pine 2 by 6, 10′ long • 1 pine 1 by 4, 6′ long
4′ of 2″ plastic pipe • 6′ of ½″ quarter-round molding • 8 flathead woodscrews, ¾″ by #8
Nylon chair glides: 4 at 1⅞″ diameter and 16 at ⅝″ diameter • Water-base powdered wood putty
1 lb. (about 200) drywall screws, 1¼″ by #6 • Wood glue • Nontoxic enamel
Automotive striping tape • Vinyl letters and numbers • 1 youth mattress, 33″ by 66″, 4″ thick

Sleek, sculptural lines belie the humble plywood origins of this dramatic race car bed. Its youth-size mattress makes it suitable for even a small bedroom. With a little time, some basic tools, and a router, you can build one for your own Grand Prix driver.

Detail 1: Plywood cutting patterns (3″ grid)

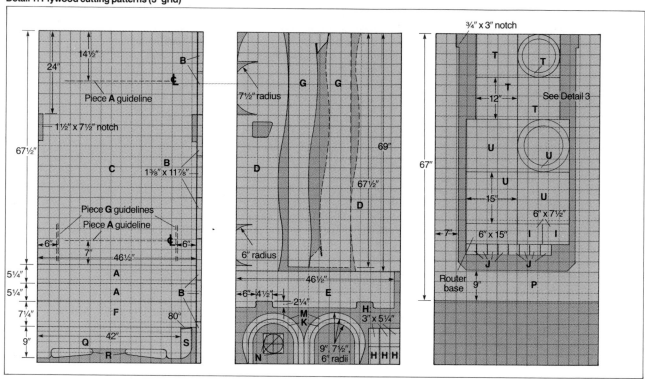

Detail 2: Nose assembly

1. Using glue, make upper and middle subassemblies from pieces cut from 6′ 2 x 6 (see drawing at bottom). Trace side profile onto ends of upper subassembly (see Detail 5); make saw cuts as shown and knock out waste area. Round over edges of middle subassembly as indicated. Trim corners of both subassemblies to a 3″ radius (see plan view).

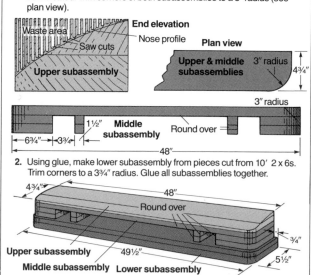

2. Using glue, make lower subassembly from pieces cut from 10′ 2 x 6s. Trim corners to a 3¾″ radius. Glue all subassemblies together.

Detail 3: Wheel routing

1. Remove router baseplate; use as a pattern to make bit and mounting holes in the plywood base. Mount router.

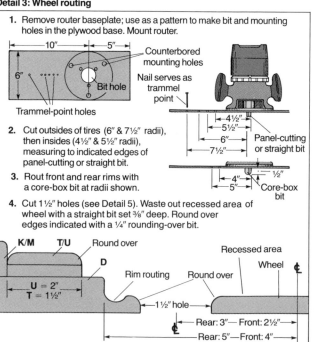

2. Cut outsides of tires (6″ & 7½″ radii), then insides (4½″ & 5½″ radii), measuring to indicated edges of panel-cutting or straight bit.

3. Rout front and rear rims with a core-box bit at radii shown.

4. Cut 1½″ holes (see Detail 5). Waste out recessed area of wheel with a straight bit set ⅜″ deep. Round over edges indicated with a ¼″ rounding-over bit.

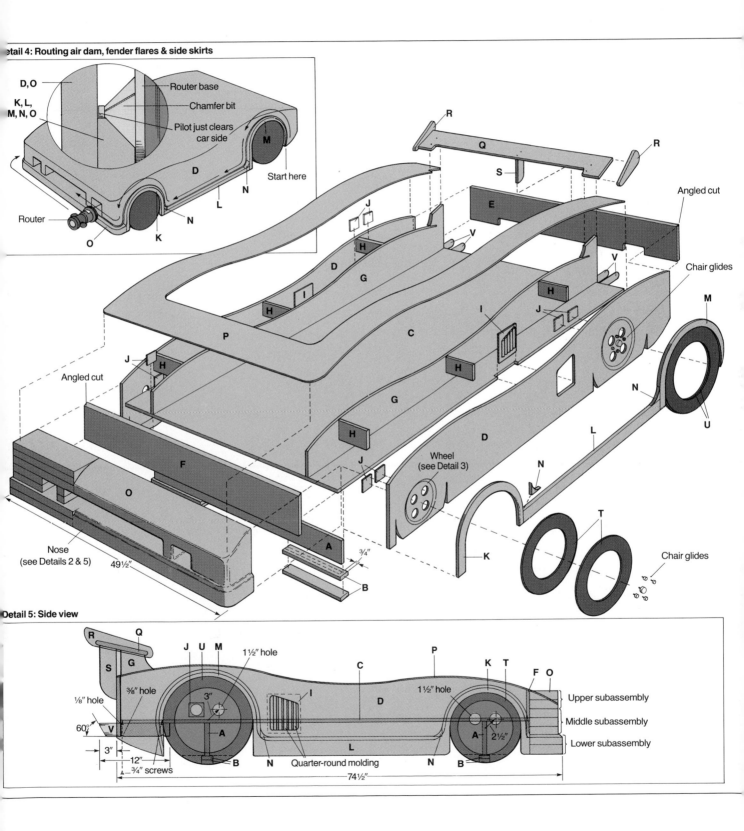

Detail 4: Routing air dam, fender flares & side skirts

D, O

K, L,
M, N, O

Router base

Chamfer bit

Pilot just clears
car side

D

M

Start here

Router

O

K

N

L

N

R

Q

R

S

E

V

V

J   J

H

D

G

I

H

P

J

H

C

I

H

J

H

G

Angled cut

H

G

D

J

F

O

A

B

Nose
(see Details 2 & 5)

49½″

Wheel
(see Detail 3)

Angled cut

Chair glides

M

N

U

L

N

K

T

Chair glides

¾″

Detail 5: Side view

R

Q

S   G

J U M

1½″ hole

I

P

C

K T

F O

1½″ hole

D

Upper subassembly

Middle subassembly

Lower subassembly

⅛″ hole

⅜″ hole

3″

A

60°

V

3″

12″

¾″ screws

B

N

Quarter-round molding

L

N   B

A   2½″

74½″

85

Occupying little more space than a twin bed, this multipurpose structure provides room for sleep, study, and storage. The elevated bed is low enough to ensure sitting headroom for older children, the adjustable desktop has ample area for serious study, and the handy wardrobe catches the closet overflow.

Teen loft bed with desk & wardrobe

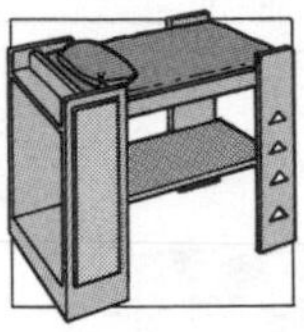

Maximize a teenager's room with this all-in-one environment. In little more space than that taken by a twin bed, this structure offers a broad desk, several shelves, closet space, and a lofty twin bed.

For this project, you'll need basic tools, a saber saw, and a radial-arm or table saw. Use a plug cutter to cut the plugs from scrap wood.

Refer to the drawings on pages 88–89 as you work.

1. Cut all pieces to size. For the fir plywood, no layouts are needed—cut platform **O** and desk top **P** from one sheet each, then cut cleats **K**, **L**, **N**, **Q**, and **R** from the remaining pieces.

Round the upper corners of closet sides **A** and uprights **E** at the radius shown in Detail 2. Cut the triangular ladder holes in one upright **E** (see Detail 2). Cut the screen molding to fit across the horizontal edge of each triangular hole and attach the pieces with brads.

Notch the corners of closet back **B** as shown in the cutting layout. Also notch both ends of notched rail **J** to fit over side rails **H** as shown.

2. To assemble the closet cabinet, glue and nail closet base **C** to two supports **D**. Then glue and screw closet back **B** to support **D**, using 2-inch screws. Glue and screw closet sides **A** to back **B** and supports **D**.

3. To assemble the other side, glue and nail one shelf **G** to two supports **D**. Glue and screw end support **F** to support **D**, then add uprights **E** (be sure to place the upright with the cutouts on the side of the bed that will face forward). Screw remaining shelf **G** in position as shown.

4. For the bed frame, round one end of each side rail **H** at the radius shown. Glue and screw end rail **I** into the side rails, using 3½-inch screws. Countersink the screws. Glue and nail cleats **K** and **L** onto the inner faces of side rails **H** and end rail **I**. Glue and screw through rails **H** into bed supports **M** as shown. Countersink the screws. Measure, then cut and attach short cleats **N** with nails.

5. Nail platform **O** to the cleats and bed supports. Screw through rails **H** into notched rail **J**, resting the lower edge of **J** on the platform support.

6. Determine the desired desk height. Then drill holes for carriage bolts through remaining two supports **D**, back **B**, and end support **F** as shown. Attach the supports with carriage bolts.

7. Glue and nail desk cleats **Q** and **R** around the edge of desk top **P**. Apply the plastic laminate to the desk top with contact cement and trim the edges (for instructions, see page 73). Drill countersink and pilot holes in desk trim **S**. Attach the trim.

8. Drill holes for the carriage bolts that connect the uprights to the bed frame. Drill counterbore holes inside the frame for the washers and nuts.

9. Plug all screw holes. Set all nails and fill the holes. Sand as required. Seal, then apply two coats of paint to all outer plywood surfaces as shown in Detail 2. Finish remaining areas with two coats of clear finish, sanding between the coats.

10. With a helper, move the components into the room. Lay the end cabinets on their sides and bolt the bed frame to them. Stand the assembly upright. Bolt the desk in place and add the mattress. Attach the closet pole end brackets; trim and add the closet pole. Mount the mirror where shown in Detail 2.

Design: Don Vandervort.

BUY		TO MAKE		
Birch plywood (shop grade)				
3	¾-inch 4 by 8-foot sheets	Pieces **A–C** and **E–G** (see Detail 1)		
Clear pine or Douglas fir				
3	8-foot 2 by 8s	2	Side rails **H**:	1½″ by 7¼″ by 85″
		1	End rail **I**:	1½″ by 7¼″ by 43½″
		1	Notched rail **J**:	1½″ by 7¼″ by 43½″
4	8-foot 2 by 3s	6	Supports **D**:	1½″ by 2½″ by 43½″
		2	Bed supports **M**:	1½″ by 2½″ by 40½″
1	6-foot 1 by 2	1	Desk trim **S**:	¾″ by 1½″ by 62⅝″
Fir plywood (grade AD)				
2	¾-inch 4 by 8-foot sheets	2	Cleats **K**:	¾″ by 1½″ by 62⅝″
		1	Cleat **L**:	¾″ by 1½″ by 40½″
		2	Cleats **N**:	¾″ by 1½″—cut to length
		1	Platform **O**:	¾″ by 40½″ by 85″
		1	Desk top **P**:	¾″ by 42¾″ by 63⅜″
		2	Desk cleats **Q**:	¾″ by 1½″ by 39¾″
		2	Desk cleats **R**:	¾″ by 1½″ by 63⅜″

MISCELLANEOUS

4′ of ¼″ by ¾″ screen molding • 4′ of 1⅜″ closet pole round

Closet pole end brackets with screws • Brads • 4d finishing nails • 2″ by #6 drywall screws

3½″ by #8 drywall screws • 4′ by 6′ sheet of plastic laminate

20 carriage bolts, ¼″ by 2″, with nuts and washers

Contact cement • Wood glue • Wood putty • Enamel • Clear penetrating oil finish

1 twin mattress, 39″ by 75″ • 15½″ by 55½″ framed mirror with mounting cleats or 4 ¾″ screws

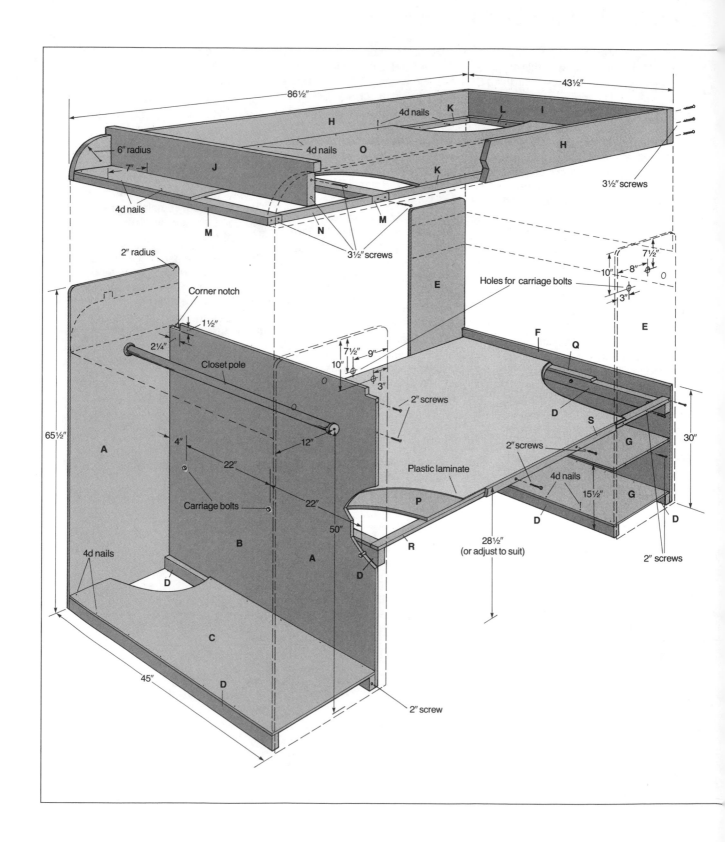

86½"

43½"

4d nails

H   K   L   I

6" radius   4d nails   O   H

7"   K

J

4d nails   3½" screws

M

M   N   M

3½" screws

2" radius

Corner notch

1½"

2¼"

7½"   8"   7½"

Closet pole   Holes for carriage bolts   10"

E

3"

O

65½"   4"   7½"   9"

12"   10"

E

22"   3"

F   Q

A   Carriage bolts   2" screws

D

S

22"   2" screws   G

50"   B   P   2" screws   4d nails   30"

A   D   15½"   G

D   R   Plastic laminate   D

D

4d nails   28½"   D

(or adjust to suit)   2" screws

C

45"   D

2" screw

Detail 1: Plywood cutting layout

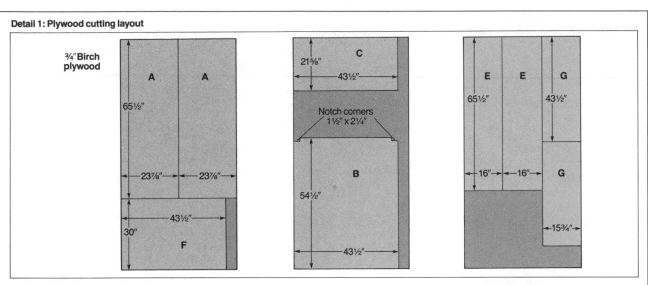

¾" Birch plywood

A A
65½"
23⅞" 23⅞"

30"
43½"
F

C
21⅝"
43½"
Notch corners
1½" x 2¼"
B
54½"
43½"

E E G
65½" 43½"
16" 16"
G
15¾"

Detail 2: Paint & ladder layout (front elevation)

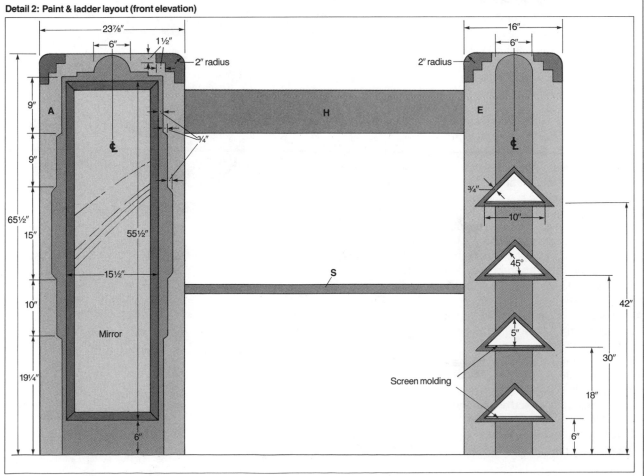

23⅞"
6" 1½"
2" radius

16"
6"
2" radius

9"
A
¾"
H
E
¾"

9"
€
€

65½"
15"
55½"
10"
45°

15½"
S
42"

10"
5"

Mirror
30"

Screen molding
18"

19¼"
6"
6"

A ROOM THAT GROWS UP

Adjustable table (below)
Crib-to-youth bed (page 92)
Adjustable desk (page 95)

Adjustable table

This easy-to-make table adjusts quickly to three different heights, making it useful for all ages, toddler to adult. A sturdy hardwood frame "tumbles" into three positions and supports an easy-care plastic laminate top.

All you'll need to build the table is a basic tool kit. One note on materials: Though we list the cross-sectional size of the frame pieces as ¾ inch by 1½ inches, available hardwood is likely to be fractionally different. Use any similar size for your table; just keep the overall dimensions accurate.

1. Cut pieces **A–D** to size. Cut the dowel into 32 pieces, each 1⅜ inches long. From the 1 by 1 pine or fir, cut eight positioning blocks, each 2¾ inches long. Cut a piece from the plastic laminate 33 inches square.

2. Glue and blind dowel frame pieces **A** to frame pieces **B**, as shown in the large drawing and Detail 1 (see page 45). Join the **AB** assemblies by gluing and through doweling (see page 44) frame connectors **C** where shown.

3. Apply the plastic laminate to table top **D** with contact cement and trim the edges (for instructions, see page 73). A bevelled trim cut is also fine; it leaves an attractive "reveal" around the table top once the edging is applied. Mark and cut trim pieces **E** for either miter or butt joints as desired; then glue and nail the trim in place. Set the nails and fill the holes.

4. Round or chamfer all the edges, sand, and apply a finish of your choice (we used lacquer).

5. Invert the top, center the frame in its lowest position (see Detail 2), and trace its outline. Mark the locations for the positioning blocks and double check their locations by trying the frame in its other positions. Glue the blocks in place.

Design: Scott Fitzgerrell.

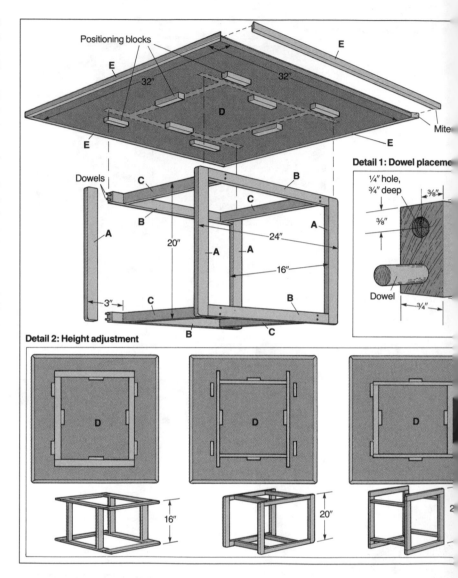

Positioning blocks

E

32"

D

32"

E

E

Miter

Dowels

C

B

C

B

B

A

A

A

A

A

20"

24"

16"

3"

C

B

C

B

C

Detail 1: Dowel placement

¼" hole, ¾" deep

⅜"

⅜"

Dowel

¾"

Detail 2: Height adjustment

D

D

D

16"

20"

BUY		TO MAKE		
Maple or birch				
Random-length 1 by 2s		4	Frame pieces **A**:	¾" by 1½" by 20"
		4	Frame pieces **B**:	¾" by 1½" by 21"
		4	Frame connectors **C**:	¾" by 1½" by 14½"
Random-length 1 by 1s		4	Trim pieces **E**:	⅞" by ⅞" by 34"
Particleboard				
1	¾-inch 4 by 4-foot sheet	1	Table top **D**:	32" by 32"

MISCELLANEOUS

4' by 4' sheet of plastic laminate • 2' of 1 by 1 pine or fir • 48" of ¼" hardwood dowel
Contact cement • 3d finishing nails • Wood glue • Wood putty • Clear nontoxic finish

All three of these cleverly designed pieces can be tailored to fit a child from infancy right through high school and beyond. In this baby's room, the adjustable table rests in its lowest position; the crib-to-youth bed is configured as a crib, with its dresser resting on the mattress support and the crib rails in place; and the adjustable desk is set in its high position, allowing an adult to work close by baby's side. For a look into the future, see page 94.

Crib-to-youth bed

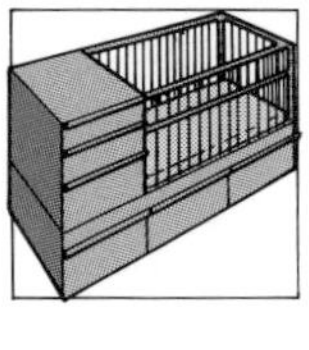

Both sleep and storage are provided for in this well-designed crib-to-youth bed. For baby, the bed is fitted with rails and a crib-size mattress. A stack of drawers nestles at the foot of the bed.

When your child outgrows the crib, the rails come off, the drawer stack moves to the floor, and—with the addition of a bunk-size mattress—the set serves through the teen-age years.

In addition to basic tools, you'll need a radial-arm or table saw equipped with a dado blade.

1. Cut all pieces to size. Cut a ¾-inch by ⅜-inch rabbet in one short edge of each cabinet side **I**. Cut 1½-inch by ¾-inch corner notches in both ends of interior supports **G**. Cut ½-inch-wide by ¼-inch-deep dadoes in drawer sides **N** (see Detail 1 and large drawing).

Cut a ¾-inch by 2-inch rabbet in the end of each post **R**. Rip one rail **U** in half and mortise for hinges where shown. Mark and drill ⅝-inch-diameter by ½-inch-deep holes for dowels in rails **S**, **T**, and **U** where shown (mark the rails together, side by side). Note: For safety, be sure to follow the specifications in the large drawing for the spacing of the dowel bars.

2. Unless otherwise specified, glue and nail all joints, spacing nails 4 to 6 inches apart. First attach sides **A** to back **B**, then to front panel **C**. Add bed cleats **D** and **E**, positioning them 2¾ inches down from the top edges. Add cleats **F** to the inner surfaces of sides **A**. Attach interior supports **G**. Add mattress support **H** and fasten it to **D**, **E**, and **G**.

3. Attach cabinet sides **I** to top **J**; then add cabinet back **K**. Add bases **L** and **M** (the base projects 2 inches below cabinet pieces **I**), fastening as shown. Mark and cut the plastic laminate to fit over top **J**. Attach it with contact cement and trim the edges (for instructions, see page 73).

4. Assemble the six drawers as shown in the large drawing and Detail 1; cut the drawer pulls from the ¾-inch stock and bevel them as shown. Mount the drawer glides, following the manufacturer's directions and allowing ⅛-inch clearance between cabinet drawers. Add casters to the bottoms of the underbed drawers.

5. Glue bars **V**, **W**, **X**, and **Y** into their respective rails as shown in the large drawing; be sure the specified length of the bars is left exposed for each panel. Fasten rails **S** to posts **R** with glue and countersunk 3-inch screws as shown. Add the hinges to the front rails where shown.

6. Set the nails and fill the holes. Sand and finish the bed and cabinet with sealer and two coats of nontoxic enamel. Use a clear nontoxic finish on the crib rail assembly and drawer pulls. Let the finish dry.

7. Remove the drawers and place the cabinet on the bed in the room where it goes. Drill counterbore holes in posts **R** for screws where shown; then screw —but don't glue—the end rail assembly to the front and back assemblies, using 2-inch screws as shown. Screw through cabinet base **L** into the ends of long rails **T**, using 2-inch screws as shown. Add the sliding bolts and their strike plates. Set in the crib mattress and put the drawers in their places.

Design: Don Vandervort.

BUY		TO MAKE		
Birch plywood (shop grade)				
2	¾-inch 4 by 8-foot sheets	Pieces **A–C**, **G**, **I–M**, and **Q** (see Detail 2)		
Fir plywood (grade AB)				
1	¾-inch 4 by 8-foot sheet	2	Bed cleats **D**:	¾" by 1¼" by 31½"
		2	Bed cleats **E**:	¾" by 1¼" by 76"
		2	Cleats **F**:	¾" by 1¼" by 9½"
		1	Mattress support **H**:	¾" by 31½" by 77½"
2	½-inch 4 by 8-foot sheets	Pieces **N–P** (see Detail 2)		
Clear fir, birch, or maple				
1	6-foot 2 by 2	2	Crib posts **R**:	1½" by 1½" by 32"
3	10-foot 2 by 2s	2	Crib rails **S**:	1½" by 1½" by 28½"
		2	Crib rails **T**:	1½" by 1½" by 54½"
		3	Crib rails **U**:	1½" by 1½" by 53¾"
Hardwood dowel				
53	⅝-inch by 36-inch lengths	21	Long front bars **V**:	⅝" by 20½"
		21	Short front bars **W**:	⅝" by 9"
		11	End bars **X**:	⅝" by 28"
		21	Back bars **Y**:	⅝" by 30"

MISCELLANEOUS

14' of ¾" by ¾" clear fir, birch, or maple • 3d finishing nails • 1" by #6 drywall screws
1½" by #6 drywall screws • 2" by #8 drywall screws • 3" by #8 drywall screws
2 2" brass butt hinges • 2 brass sliding bolts • 3 pairs of 22" full-extension drawer glides
12 1¾" plate-mounted casters with screws • Contact cement • Sealer
23¾" by 31½" sheet of plastic laminate • Wood glue • Wood putty • Clear nontoxic finish
Nontoxic enamel • Crib-size mattress, 27¼" by 52", or bunk-size mattress, 30" by 75"

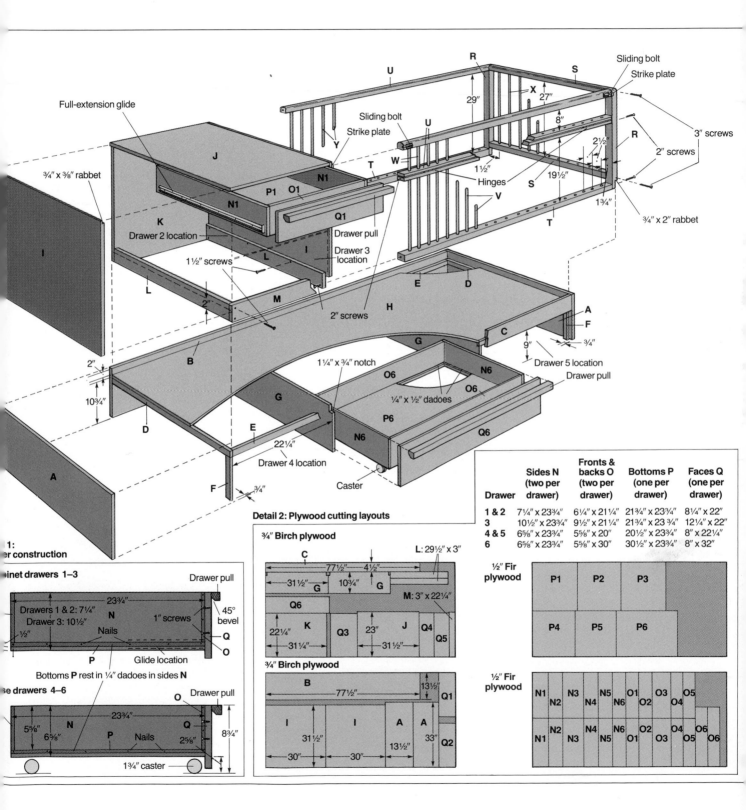

Full-extension glide

¾″ x ⅜″ rabbet

R U S Sliding bolt
Strike plate
29″ X 27″
8″
Sliding bolt U
Strike plate 2½″
J T W R
N1 3″ screws
P1 O1 1½″ 2″ screws
N1 Hinges 19½″
K Q1 S
Drawer 2 location Drawer pull 1¾″
I I L Drawer 3 T ¾″ x 2″ rabbet
1½″ screws location
L E D
M H A
2″ 2″ screws C F
B G 9″ ¾″
I A Drawer 5 location
Drawer pull
2″ 1¼″ x ¾″ notch O6 N6
10¾″ ¼″ x ½″ dadoes O6
G P6
D E N6 Q6
22¼″
A N6
Drawer 4 location
F ¾″ Caster

Detail 2: Plywood cutting layouts

	Sides N (two per drawer)	Fronts & backs O (two per drawer)	Bottoms P (one per drawer)	Faces Q (one per drawer)
Drawer				
1 & 2	7¼″ x 23¾″	6¼″ x 21¼″	21¾″ x 23¾″	8¼″ x 22″
3	10½″ x 23¾″	9½″ x 21¼″	21¾″ x 23 ¾″	12¼″ x 22″
4 & 5	6⅝″ x 23¾″	5⅝″ x 20″	20½″ x 23¾″	8″ x 22¼″
6	6⅝″ x 23¾″	5⅝″ x 30″	30½″ x 23¾″	8″ x 32″

¾″ Birch plywood

C L: 29½″ x 3″
77½″ 4½″
31½″ G 10¾″ G
G M: 3″ x 22¼″
Q6
22¼″ K Q3 23″ J Q4
31¼″ 31½″ Q5

¾″ Birch plywood

B 13½″
77½″ Q1
I I A A 33″ Q2
31½″ 13½″
30″ 30″

½″ Fir plywood

P1 P2 P3
P4 P5 P6

½″ Fir plywood

N1 N3 N5 O1 O3 O5
N2 N4 N6 O2 O4
N2 N4 N6 O2 O4 O6
N1 N3 N5 O1 O3 O5 O6

1:
er construction

inet drawers 1–3
Drawer pull
23¾″ 45°
Drawers 1 & 2: 7¼″ N bevel
Drawer 3: 10½″ 1″ screws
Nails Q
½″ O
P Glide location
Bottoms P rest in ¼″ dadoes in sides N

se drawers 4–6
O Drawer pull
23¾″
5⅝″ N Q
6⅝″ 8¾″
P Nails 2⅝″
1¾″ caster

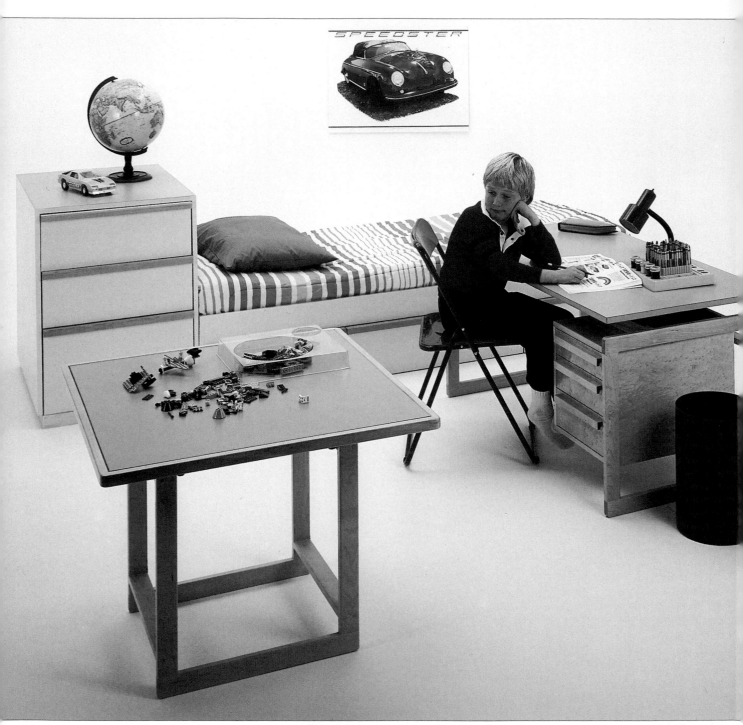

As the child grows, the furniture can be adjusted to fit. In a grade schooler's room, the three-position table is set in its highest configuration for model building (it changes quickly to its other positions as needed); the crib-to-youth bed has been separated into its dresser and bed components; and the adjustable desk (in its low position) is at a comfortable height for the young scholar.

Adjustable desk

To adjust this handy desk, simply rotate the two-way frame and reposition the cabinet and the top.

You'll need basic tools and a router, radial-arm saw, or table saw. Note: Our 1 by 2 maple measured ¾ inch by 1½ inches. If yours differs, just keep the overall dimensions accurate.

1. Cut pieces **A–J** to size (see the materials list and drawings). Cut 32 dowel pieces, each 1⅜ inches long. Bevel drawer pulls **J**. Cut dadoes and rabbets in the drawer and cabinet pieces (see the detail drawing). From the 1 by 4, cut positioning blocks; cut a stop block and drawer runners from scrap.

2. Glue and blind dowel (see page 45) frame pieces **A** to pieces **B**; glue and through dowel (see page 44) the **AB** assemblies to frame connectors **C**.

3. Glue and nail together pieces D, E, and F. Assemble pieces G, H, and I (see the detail drawing). Attach pulls J. With the cabinet on its back, position the drawers, leaving 1/16 inch around each one. Mark the location of each drawer-side dado on the cabinet. Glue and nail the runners on these marks.

4. From the particleboard, cut desk top **K** to size. Glue and nail the positioning blocks to **K**. From the laminate, cut one piece at 27 by 48 inches, two at 1 by 27 inches, and two at 1 by 48 inches. Apply to the top and edges of **K** with contact cement (see page 73).

5. Round or chamfer all wood edges, fill the holes, sand, and finish as desired. Turn the frame upside down in the "tall" position. Position the cabinet and drill two pilot holes through the top into each connector **C**. Repeat in the "short" position, using the holes as guides for drilling remaining connectors **C**. Mount the cabinet with 2-inch screws, set the top in place, and glue the stop block to the cabinet top.

Design: Helge Olsen.

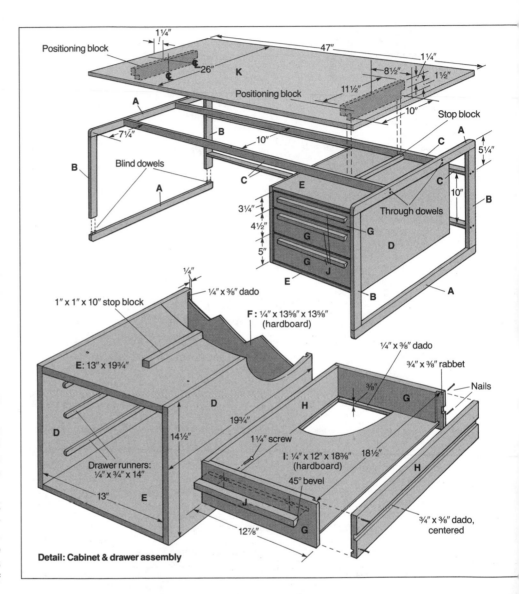

Detail: Cabinet & drawer assembly

BUY		TO MAKE		
Birch or maple				
Random-length 1 by 2s		4	Frame pieces **A**:	¾" by 1½" by 26"
		4	Frame pieces **B**:	¾" by 1½" by 19"
		4	Frame connectors **C**:	¾" by 1½" by 44½"
		3	Drawer pulls **J**:	¾" by 1" by 11"

MISCELLANEOUS

¾" Baltic birch plywood, 5' by 5' • ¼" hardboard, 4' by 4' • ¾" particleboard, 4' by 4'
48" by 48" sheet of plastic laminate • 2' of 1 by 4 pine or fir
#6 drywall screws: 6 at 1¼", 4 at 2" • 48" of ¼" hardwood dowel • 3d finishing nails
Wood glue • Contact cement • Wood putty • Clear nontoxic finish

INDEX